Fishers and Hunters

Meridel Rawlings

Abridged Edition

International Vistas Inc.
P.O. Box 8232
Jerusalem
Israel

New Wine Press
P.O. Box 17
Chichester
England

Fishers and Hunters
British Edition jointly published with:
New Wine Press
P.O. Box 17
Chichester
England

ISBN 0 947852 11 5

Printed and bound in Great Britain by
Anchor Brendon Ltd, Tiptree, Essex

Contents

Acknowledgments

Gratefully I recognize the thousands upon thousands of unsung heroes, Jew and Christian alike, who over the centuries, have cherished the Word of God, waiting by faith for the day which is now upon us. History repeatedly reminds us of the activity of the Hunters, but we must never forget the gentle Fishers who have always set a standard of righteousness in the earth by attempting to "love their neighbours as themselves".[1]

My special thanks to Jenny Sun, Laura Tuin, Laurel Dawe, Eleanor Fisher and Janice Booth, for helping to type the manuscript at various stages. Also to Ya'acov Polak for his technical advice and to my husband and Robert Amoyles for their editorial comments.

I praise the Lord for my husband, Jay, who so willingly shares his loving faith and vision with us, his family. We are encouraged to listen to and obey the "still small voice".

And . . . to "The Holy One of Israel", for speaking, and inspiring.

---

[1] Leviticus 19:18
Luke 10:27

Foreword

If God were to take you to His treasure house and give you your choice, what would it be? Mine would be an ear to hear His voice, being able to know every moment of my life, "I am where He wants me to be, doing what He wants me to do."

If this is the great desire of your heart, this book is for you. The writer and her husband—dear, dear friends of mine—have this most precious of gifts beyond almost anyone I know. They have made the great discovery—how to let Jesus live His life through them, speak through their lips, look out through their eyes, reach out through their hands—to a very special people—His brethren.

To walk with them—and this has been my privilege in places near and far—is to walk with Jesus, and to talk, to laugh, and to sing with Him.

I invite you to walk with them and Him in the pages of this book. You will find yourself in unimaginable places, doing and saying unimaginable things, all the while knowing He is living His life through you. Your life will never be the same, because you will not be.

HARALD BREDESEN

Preface

> And when ye see this, your heart shall rejoice, and your bones shall flourish like an herb....[1]

> ...and I will bring them again into their land that I gave unto their fathers.
> Behold, I will send for many fishers, saith the Lord, and they shall fish them; and after will I send for many hunters, and they shall hunt them from every mountain, and from every hill, and out of the holes of the rocks.[2]

Over 2500 years ago the prophets of Israel forecast the ingathering of the Jews and the rebuilding of their nation in the Land of Israel. Today living in Israel are 3½ million Jews from over 100 nations of the world. By this immigration, particularly during the last 60 years, we know the Holy Spirit is doing this work as promised. Israel as a modern nation was born after the tragic loss of six million Jews in the death camps of the Nazi Holocaust. Perhaps Jeremiah foresaw this systematic murder by the Nazis and the subsequent rise of worldwide terrorist activity and referred to them as "hunters"?

"I will send for many fishers..." is the other portion of that prophetic word. Fishermen are quiet and gentle; in this case their desire is to catch the "fish" and see them transferred from the great rivers of the world, so to speak, back to their

---

[1] Isaiah 66:14.

[2] Jeremiah 16:15–16.

spawning ground where they belong—Israel. The Scriptures clearly teach that after the fishers, again the hunters will come, and we see evidence of this daily in our newspapers. Anti-Semitism and anti-Zionism are on the rise. This is just one of the signs of the times in which we are living. Israel's enemies will make sure that the Jews will be blamed for the economic disasters soon to befall our society. A provision has been made for the Jews as a people in this generation, and that provision is Israel.

This book is a series of personal encounters. All experiences and conversations have taken place. Some names and circumstances have been changed to protect individual privacy.

The 'fishers' have dared to reach across the barbed wire of Church history and tradition to touch the Jew in blessing. In the love of the Living God, they have said to our Jewish brothers and sisters: "We are sorry for the cold facts of history, because everything that we hold precious in life has come from God through you, the Holy Scriptures and Jesus Himself."

Surprise and delight were our portion many times as unexpected circumstances led us to speak to the various individuals in these stories. We were reminded of the unconventional method by which Peter was led to Cornelius' house, so that the blessing given first to the Jew could be shared by the Jews to the Gentiles.[3] Likewise, we were constantly aware of the Holy Spirit as our wise sage and guide during these episodes, in which the blessings that we have enjoyed for so long enabled us to reach out to Jews in various parts of the world. Some may find occasion for criticism; if this is the case, perhaps they need to be reminded that Jesus said, "If ye have done it unto one of the least of these *My* brethren, ye have done it unto Me."[4]

---

[3] Acts 10:25–31.

[4] Matthew 25:40b.

Good Jewish mommas, presidents of Hebrew communities, sabras, a kosher butcher, a psychiatrist, along with a victim of terror and survivors of the Holocaust, make a bright collage of characters. Together we generate a lot of sound and light, but when tempered by the fire of the Spirit of God, the sweetest of all music is produced. To know our spiritual inheritance is to discover the greatest of life's treasures, whether we be Jew or Christian.

The 'fishers' you will meet in the pages of this book are a wide variety of characters from many different walks of life.

Vee Gardner is a Philadelphia lawyer's widow. At 43 years of age she found her grief turned to joy in her desire to bless the Jewish communities around her.

Doug Phillips, a young Californian, spent a year in Jerusalem studying Hebrew. The following summer he visited the death camps of Europe to gain a clearer understanding of the awful truth concerning the Holocaust. Doug opened his heart and life to bless and not curse the Jew.

Impetuous Rick Alvarez is a bundle of energy and under the direction of the Holy Spirit left the Mount Sinai Hospital in New York to visit various Jewish communities around the world. His Iberian ancestry is easily discernible through his Spanish accent.

Edward Hull was a chain-smoking, hard-driving American businessman for years. Then he met Jesus in a personal way. The once hard lines on his face today are kindly wrinkles. He's in big business in God's service, with the Holy Spirit as his executive director.

Julia Tooley at 17 years of age was bored with private schools in New Zealand. She received permission from her parents to spend two years abroad. Little did anyone realize that this young lady would visit 18 rabbis in South Africa alone, and bless many Jews in Europe and Israel before she died in a car accident at 20 years of age.

Krista Barten, from Virginia, once a shy secretary with flaxen hair and blue eyes, had many unique opportunities to pour oil upon troubled waters among the Jewish people.

Jill Douglas, head nurse of an intensive care unit for 12 years, learned what it meant "to be directed by the Holy Spirit" while on vacation in Europe. Jill now nurses in a Hebrew-speaking hospital in Israel.

Ivy Flynn, psychiatric nurse, scuba diver and pilot, sought and found adventure by sharing ancient biblical promises with a psychiatrist, architect and Russian Jews.

Sheila Kedwell, nutritionist major, watched her carefully planned world fall to pieces when her husband walked out with another woman. You will chuckle and smile at the way the Creator used Sheila to confound and comfort the wise.

Beth Tanner, from south of the Mason–Dixon line, found her soul music and visionary faith instrumental in the hands of the Master Planner behind the Iron Curtain.

Yossi Hochman, an Israeli, shares his tragic story. He was the sole survivor of his family in a terrorist bus incident in Israel, in which he lost his legs.

Jay and Meridel Rawlings, Canadian nurse and hospital administrator, laid aside their professions, financial security and the comfort of convention to follow the divine challenge given them: "If you love Me, love My people."[5] Over the last 14 years they have coursed 90 nations by faith, searching out Jewish communities, pointing them to Israel. They have also spoken to various churches in those nations declaring the absolute necessity of Christian support for Israel, and the local Jew. 'Home,' they learned, was wherever they happened to be, until Passover 1976 when they came to settle in Israel. Today, living in Jerusalem, they continue to pour their time and energies into the work of "comforting Zion." Well-known guests on Canada's daily Christian television program, "100 Huntley Street," they are able to share many facets of life in Israel.

As researcher and co-producer of the film, "Apples of

---

[5] Matthew 25:40b.

Gold," they worked closely together with many dedicated individuals who labored tirelessly behind the scenes, filming in Israel and later in post-production at the "100 Huntley Street" studios in Toronto. Premiered in Jerusalem, February 1980, this "factual and artistic docu-drama" traces the last seventy years of Israel's history. Key Israelis who took part in shaping modern Israel share some of their experiences.

The 80's, called by some "the fright decade," ushered in a new era of intensified action for or against Israel, when overnight Jerusalem became the center of world attention. On July 30, 1980, the Israeli Parliament passed the Jerusalem Law, which states: "Jerusalem, in her entirety, is the capital of Israel." Immediately the U.N. took a firm stand against this declaration and as a result all existing embassies in Jerusalem were moved to Tel Aviv. Failure to comply meant severed oil supplies. International blackmail became an accepted tool in the hand of the 'hunters.'

In response, thanks to the initiative and courage of a handful of 'fishers,' the International Christian Embassy was opened in Jerusalem on September 30, 1980. Today, through its numerous branches in many nations, the Embassy has become a significant voice on behalf of Israel. An awakening towards Israel is taking place among Christians worldwide. Thousands come annually to Jerusalem to participate in the 'Christian Celebration of the Feast of Tabernacles.'

Since then, in light of current world events a revised fourth edition of "Fishers and Hunters" has been produced. Recent happenings in the Soviet Union and in Ethiopia have signalled a new and challenging relevance of prophecy.

The Bible speaks clearly about the ingathering of the outcasts of Israel. In Isaiah chapter 43, verse 5 for example it says: "I will say to the north, give up and to the south keep not back: bring my sons from far and my daughters from the ends of the earth."

Since 1983 one of the lost tribes of Israel, the Ethiopian Jews, began their return to Zion en masse. With their origins shrouded in mystery, they call themselves the 'Beta Israel' or 'House of Israel', and are thought to be descendants of King Solomon.

Their partial exodus has been both miraculous and complicated and so we felt it appropriate to include a chapter on them in this edition. They need our prayers so that the SOUTH WILL KEEP NOT BACK the eighteen thousand who still remain, their future uncertain in the famine and disease stricken nation of Marxist Ethiopia.

On the other hand, Russian Jews and their plight has also become the focus of attention to students of Bible prophecy. Recently they have been the object of horrific anti-semitic attacks reminiscent of Nazi Germany. Currently the situation is such that Kremlin watchers are now describing their conditions as distinctly neo-Stalinist. In response and following three personal visits to the Soviet Jews in Russia, we have produced a film and book by the same title: "Gates of Brass". It is our prayer that through these documents new understanding will arise in men of goodwill everywhere and that action will result, when we together stand up and say to the north, "GIVE UP!"

In "Fishers and Hunters" you will meet 'watchmen' who being aware of the significance of the day in which we live, have stepped out of the prescribed mould called 'tradition' to bless and not only comfort, but fight for the rights of our Jewish people by acting and speaking a word 'in season' to this generation.

All scripture is quoted from the King James version of the Bible unless otherwise stated.

Jerusalem, June 1985

Jay Rawlings
Meridel Rawlings
ARGENTINA

1
The Bridge

It was May and the sunshine, heavy with moisture, made the heat unbearable. My husband Jay and I were already late for our appointment. Besides that, we had standing room only on the crowded bus, and frustation enveloped us when the bus came to a complete standstill locked in a traffic jam. Still, I was looking forward to meeting the Rabbi and willingly withstood the rigors of travel in the late months of my pregnancy. Beads of perspiration gathered on my upper lip.

Finally we arrived at the steps of the ultra-Orthodox stone synagogue, puffing and wet. It was inexcusable to keep such an important man waiting.

The Hassidic Rabbi was of Eastern European origin. He was a large man, big boned and very brisk in his manner. His eyes were black as night and surveyed us coolly. He puffed nervously away at his cigarette. Having entered the sanctuary of his study, he began in a thick accent, "You're Christians!" It wasn't a compliment!

"Yes," Jay cleared his throat, only to be interrupted.

"I hate you," the words were spat at us. "I don't want anything to do with you! All Christians have done for us is cause us harm and reproach. TROUBLE—that's what you are—TROUBLE!" The Rabbi was white with anger. "I just don't want anything to do with you!" His words were barely whispered. The room became very quiet. He stood, suddenly at a loss for words, and then began in a more controlled voice.

"So, why have you come to talk to Jews? You have obviously suffered from these travels!" He eyed me large with child. "Why? What would encourage you to such a life? Why don't you visit the Catholics or the Indians? They need your help."

Mentally I ducked the barrage of words and held my peace. This Rabbi must see that we were his friends. Not wanting to suffer a woman to speak, he informed me of the many Hassidic customs concerning the place of women. He included the fact that a holy man would not even shake hands with a woman. Why he was lecturing us like this I couldn't imagine. I listened as an obedient wife.

"I understand," Jay broke in slowly, "we do not take offence when people such as yourself say you don't like Christians. Why should you? We don't have a very good track record in history. I understand perfectly. Will you forgive us?" he asked quietly. The piercing, hateful look left the Rabbi's eyes.

"Some are different," Jay continued. "We have learned to love and obey the Lord and He in turn has blessed us abundantly. His blessing came to us with an overflowing love for the Jews and with an understanding of the vital role that they play in the earth today according to the Bible. We believe the promises given by the prophets. He *is* gathering His people home to Israel."

"Please sit down, sit down," the Rabbi spoke hurriedly, a little embarrassed that we were all still standing. His manner was brisk, but the hostility was gone. "Yes, please continue," he nodded his shiny domed head as if to encourage Jay to continue.

"As you know," Jay chose his words carefully, "the word Christian in Hebrew is Notzri, 'watchman'." Again the shiny head nodded, this time in agreement. He seemed pleased that we knew a little Hebrew. "We have chosen to be watchmen with the responsibility of alerting the various Jewish and Christian communities in the earth, making them aware of the time in which they are living as related to the Land of Israel." By this time the Rabbi was listening intently, as he stroked his beard.

"Our travels to the various nations of the world, some 87 by now, have been unique! I was challenged to give up a successful career in Canada and in 1969 our hearts were deeply touched by a visit to Israel and Jerusalem. From there we travelled around the world many times—to far corners—from Tierra del Fuego to Peking, searching for the Jew, and encouraging him to return home to Israel. Meridel, my "garden enclosed"[1] from the Lord, and our sons, often travel with me. They are my greatest supporters. As parents we have learned that "home" is not a place, its being together."

"Just recently we have visited every country in South America and have spoken in synagogues to community presidents, rabbis, women's groups, shopkeepers, anyone who would listen. No large organization supports us, however private individuals who believe in the validity of our message have helped us to travel to the various communities. We also encourage and educate the local churches that they must befriend the Jews in their cities and support Israel. Gently we try to motivate the rabbis to point their people toward Israel. I'm sure you know that the Lord is doing something new in the earth. Israel is the home of a new generation. The sabra is proud of his heritage and can stand tall alongside of any other people."

"Go on—go on." The Rabbi was actually encouraging Jay to speak.

He continued, relaxed and smiling, "Perhaps one of the most trying things for us to overcome is being misunderstood. To the Christian world we are peculiar in our avid love for, and support of the Jews and Israel as their rightful homeland and Jerusalem as their capital. This is changing today, and

[1] Song of Solomon 4:12a.

to our great joy Christians are realizing the monumental importance of Israel's preservation, not for the sake of the Jew alone, but for the ultimate preservation of the millions who have their roots in the Bible. Living in nations whose government policies are in direct opposition to the existence of the nation of Israel these Bible believers want a voice.

"On the other hand, to the Jew, in the beginning the question was, 'Can they be trusted? What is their motivation?'

"How very well I remember a slight spinster in Berlin, the only survivor of her family. After eyeing me very suspiciously she said, 'This is your MISSION in life, isn't it?'

"'Well, dear,' I replied gently, 'I would call it the love of my life!'"

"How old are your children?" the Rabbi inquired, changing the subject.

It was my turn to say something, woman or not. "We have been blessed with two beautiful little boys, now ages four and two."

"Are they travelling with you?" His interest was genuine.

"Why yes," I responded, "we try to stay together as a family as much as possible, and the children are never any trouble. In fact...."

The Rabbi stopped me with, "Why would you do it? Do you really think that we don't know what you are saying?" He nodded in my direction indicating that I was to answer his query.

"Yes, of course we know that you understand the implications of what we are saying—better than we do, no doubt... but maybe you need to be reminded. You see," I hesitated, "I fell in love with a Jew." I looked at the quiet Rabbi very directly. He waited, not knowing what I was going to say. "And," I continued, "His name is Jesus, and He said, 'If you love Me, love My people.' It's very simple, but that is the truth! Remember, the Lord God of Israel loves YOU!"

Slowly, slowly, the atmosphere in the room began to change from one of cold hostility to one of acceptance. One could feel the transformation sweep in. The worry lines on the Rabbi's brow began to relax. A soft, faraway look came into his eyes, and his cigarette lay snuffed out in the ashtray.

"You must tell your people to make every preparation to return to Israel, for Israel is the only land of 'blessing' for them. They are not safe here in Argentina," Jay urged.

The first five minutes had stretched to thirty minutes, an hour, and then it was time to go. We three arose, smiling, congenial friends. Good wishes for one another came from sincere hearts. Over the heavy wooden desk Jay and the Rabbi shook hands in the warmth of friendship. To their amazement, as if propelled from within, the Rabbi then shot forth his holy Hassidic hand toward me. In response, I instantly extended my hand to him. Then, all of a sudden, as both of our hands were extended over his broad, polished desk, we stopped, frozen by tradition. The Rabbi was not permitted to so much as touch my hand, or any woman's for that matter. His kind smiling eyes met mine but his hand fell silently to his side. The gap had been bridged, for Zion heard and was glad.

Kol ha-olam kulo
Gesher tzar m'od.
V'ha-ikar, v'ha-ikar
Lo l'fached, lo l'fached clal.

All the world is a very narrow bridge.
The principal thing is not to fear.[2]

ARGENTINA

[2] Old Hebrew song and translation.

Rick Alvarez
AUSTRALIA

2
A Synagogue for Christmas

It was the 24th of December and everyone knows what that means. Instead of doing last-minute Christmas shopping, Rick Alvarez, a Portuguese from New York, left that task to his wife. He had something else in mind, for he had asked for a very special present! You see, there was only one synagogue in this small out-of-the-way town in Western Australia, and Rick's desire was to see it reopened! He headed for the tiny local Jewish community and asked to see the custodian of the synagogue.

Rick was a fast talker and took advantage of the fact that he was a tourist, by saying, "We are just here for a very short time, and it's a pity to see the synagogue totally unused."

Mr. Jacobs, the caretaker, lamented, "What's the use? We can never get a minyan together." He put the key in the rusty keyhole and the double wooden doors swung open. The air was heavy with dust as Rick peered into the once much-used sanctuary. Mice had been at work on the prayer books, and the unused state of the building gave one a lonely, sad feeling.

"How could they just leave it to fall into ruin like this?" queried Rick to himself. "Please, just turn on the lights," he encouraged Mr. Jacobs. "I'm going to ask God to visit this place," Rick announced. And much to the surprise of Mr. Jacobs, he did just that. First he began to dance and to praise the Holy One of Israel at the top of his voice. The little caretaker couldn't remember when he had heard such fervor in his synagogue. Rick continued speaking aloud in faith, "And Lord, bring ten righteous men, reopen this house and give them a Rabbi. I thank You for it and I praise You." Just as promptly as he had come, he was finished and ready to go.

As Mr. Jacobs relocked the old doors, he just didn't know what to think. "This man seems normal enough," he thought drily to himself. "What had just happened was certainly unusual, but then it takes all kinds of people to fill the world," he decided.

The following evening, December 25, found Rick and his wife attending a Charismatic worship service. Doctrinal differences that had separated Christians for centuries melted away in this congregation under the anointing of the Spirit of God. Their lives had been transformed from nominal Christianity to a people of praise and faith. This sovereign work of God was not an isolated example, but in recent years has occurred all over the earth, sweeping thousands upon thousands of believers into the experience known as the "baptism in the Holy Spirit."

Rick was among the congregation that arose in unison to sing praises to the Lord. Instruments led the way to worship in song.

> I love Thee, Lord, and I lift my voice
> To worship Thee; oh my soul, rejoice.
> Take joy, my King, in what You hear;
> May it be a sweet, sweet sound in Your ear.

The multitude of voices blended into one. Together the worship—on instruments and in vocal praise—was as the sound of many waters that rolled heavenward; mighty waves of praise ascending to the very throne of God. In response, His glory came down upon the congregation, for He was inhabiting the praises of His people. Then, as if controlled by an unseen conductor, slowly and gently the harmony of united praise subsided, until a complete silence filled the building.

One could feel the presence of the Lord God Almighty come down perceived as a blanket of peace by to those who like the prophets of old desired to hear from heaven.

At that moment a man stood to his feet, and in a loud and powerful voice he spoke out in a language foreign to everyone present. After giving the message he sat down. Seconds later, another man on the platform came to the microphone and gave the interpretation, according to the biblical pattern of the early church. Everyone listened attentively.

"'Comfort, comfort My people,' says your God. 'Speak comfortably to Jerusalem and cry to her that her warfare is accomplished. Say unto the cities of Judah, "Behold your God." Prepare the way of the Lord. And the glory of the Lord shall be revealed and all flesh shall see it together. Carry My people in your bosom as a nursing father bears the sucking child, for Ephraim is My firstborn. Let him that glories glory in this, a broken and a contrite heart I will not despise. I am the Lord, which exercises lovingkindness, judgment and righteousness in the earth. Pour your praises out before Me, pour out your prayers, and I shall in turn pour out of My goodness upon the earth.' "

Rick was sitting near the back of the congregation, humbled by the message that had just been given. It seemed just for him, with the concern and delight he carried for the Jews and for Israel.

"Yes, oh Lord, I will be pleased to comfort Your people," he prayed silently. "Just show me how." No sooner had the response of his heart been formed into thought when the gentle, truthful voice that he knew to be the Spirit of God began to speak into his heart. "A man stands outside. I have drawn him by My Spirit. Go out and speak to him. I will use him to reopen the synagogue, for he is a Jew."

Without hesitation Rick quietly got up and slipped out of the sanctuary. Sure enough, on the sidewalk in front of the steps of the church, looking indecisive, stood a man.

"Hello," Rick called out as he skipped down the front steps

two at a time, his right hand extended. "You are a Jew, aren't you?"

"Yes, but how did you know?" the man replied with a firm handshake. "I am originally from Poland and I stopped to listen, for I heard a man in there speaking Yiddish."

Rick explained, "You may find this hard to believe, but the man who spoke such fluent Yiddish does not know this language. This was the Spirit of God speaking through him. It's a gift that God gives. He was speaking in your language for you to understand."

"It's amazing, just amazing," replied the stranger, looking even more puzzled.

"May I call you by your first name?" Rick asked.

"Sure, I'm Nathaniel," he replied.

"Nathaniel, the Lord has something for you to do."

"He does? What could He possibly want me to do?"

"Yes He does, He has a special task for you. Did you know the synagogue in this town has been closed for years?"

"Yes, I'm aware of that fact," he said, looking down.

"Well, I feel you are the one the Lord has chosen to gather ten men to reopen its doors. If you will remain faithful, I believe God will send you a Rabbi in time...." His voice trailed off into a pause.

The man standing before Rick had been significantly touched. His heart had responded to the message in Yiddish, and his longing had been to see his own people restored. "How is it that this Gentile could read my thoughts?" the Jew wondered. He began to speak slowly, "How did you know? How could anyone have known that I felt this way?"

"Well," Rick answered lovingly, "God has proved it by telling me your thoughts. Before you called He has answered."[1]

"But you aren't a Jew?"

---

[1] Matthew 6:8.

"No," said Rick, "but I've come to love the Jew, Jesus, and consequently I love the Jews." He was always forthright!

"Say," responded Nathaniel, brightening, "if I get a minyan for next Shabbat, could you come and speak to us?"

"Yes, I'd be honored to." Rick was delighted! Nathaniel did not know that, just the night before, Rick had asked God to open the doors of his synagogue, and he, in turn, was opening its doors to Rick.

"Isn't this the biggest day of your year?" Nathaniel grinned.

"Why yes. Imagine you remembering that!" Rick was surprised.

"Well then, a very Merry Christmas to you and Shalom."

"Thank you and Shalom," said Rick as they parted.

One week later, the synagogue doors were open. Eleven men had come to make the minyan and to pray on behalf of themselves and their little ones. Rick Alvarez was present with them as their first guest speaker in many years.

"Not by might, nor by power, but by my spirit, saith the Lord of hosts."

Zechariah 4:6

AUSTRALIA

Doug Phillips
POLAND

3
Secluded Places

I look from my mill to see mounds of grief,
Shadows of struggles for Jewish belief,
But to no avail.
I look through a constantly turning wheel
To remember Father, but he couldn't conceal
His faith in Him.
There was dear little Shuly, but not for long;
Momma just weeps, "Poppa, what's wrong?"

Doug Phillips was just sixteen and surfacing from the drug scene in California when he was inspired to write this poem. Little did he realize that these few lines of poetry were the beginning of a road map leading him not only to Jerusalem, but to the gas chambers of Europe.

As is typical of many children born in the fifties, Doug had no first-hand knowledge of what went on in World War II, even though his father had served overseas for two years. The War was never mentioned at home. Doug had an unusual love in his young heart for Israel and her people. It was during his visit to the Holocaust Museum in Jerusalem (Yad va-Shem)[1] that he felt God had wanted his mind spared from the

[1] Yad va-Shem not only has the world's largest archives (30 million documents) and library (over 50,000 volumes) on the Holocaust, but has also published more books (over 100) on this subject than any other institute or publisher in the world.

awful truth of the War until now, when it had a depth of meaning for him. While the term Holocaust has been used by Jews and academics for a number of years, it is relatively new to most Christians. In fact, it was probably largely unknown until the television series in 1978 brought it vividly before the public.

Just a few weeks after visiting the Holocaust Museum, Doug was on his way to Europe to visit ten Nazi concentration camps.

He took a train to Krakow, a town in Poland, not far from the Czech border. From the train window he gazed out onto pastoral scenes of rolling farmlands. Doug began to hum a new tune; it arose in his heart above the clicking of the train wheels on the track.

> For the Lord hath chosen Zion;
> He hath desired it for His habitation.
> This is my rest for ever:
> Here will I dwell.
> This is my rest for ever,
> Here will I dwell.[2]

He sang softly to himself.

His first destination was a village called Oswiecim. Farmsteads had stood where the silent remains of the famous concentration camps of Auschwitz and Birkenau remain to tell their sordid story to all who will look and listen. The first thing that Doug saw after getting down from the train was the great iron gate to Auschwitz. On the top of the gate, in bold German lettering, stood the words, "Work Liberates." Auschwitz had held slave laborers. Its inmates had survived the selection process at the railway platform in Birkenau, about two miles away. First the victims had arrived in cattle-cars from all over Europe; those selected as fit to work at Auschwitz lived longer than a few hours. Upon their arrival at

[2] Psalm 132:13, 14.

Auschwitz they were stripped of everything, even their hair.

Just entering in through the gates made Doug nauseated. The camp had been left intact, with little signs featuring the skull and crossbones strategically located, with the word "HALT" beneath them.

The barrack Block 27 had been turned into a hideous museum, with gunnysacks full of human hair. Doug could smell it, and felt more nauseated. Spread before him were grotesque pictures, hair brushes and eyeglasses piled high. Other reminders of the inhumanity practiced in this place were crutches, wooden legs, suitcases with names carefully written on them, mounds of clothing, kitchen utensils, and shoes; there were even empty cans of Zyklon B gas.

Doug wandered through the camp by himself. He wanted to experience all that God would lay upon his heart. As he walked, he told the Lord that he was willing to bear the reproach of the Jew. He saw the barbed wire fences that had been charged with electricity. The watchtowers commanded a a presence, as did the dogs. Now it was all so quiet. God told Doug to weep for His Jewish people—not a pitying kind of weeping, but as a burden from His hand. It was not difficult for Doug to weep for the Jews, who had known abuse, hatred and attempts of annihilation for centuries. He wept also for affluent Jews today who are becoming assimilated. Through his tears Doug came to understand that in spite of the Holocaust, the Jewish people possessed a spirit given by God, as indestructible as God Himself.

"Thou shalt preserve them from this generation for ever."[3] Those words rang over and over in his mind, in complete contradiction to all that he was seeing and experiencing. God's word cannot lie, and in that knowledge he was comforted. Evil men lay their carefully devised plans, but God still has the ultimate word.

---

[3] Psalm 12:7.

Leaving Auschwitz, Doug walked the two miles to Birkenau. The smokestacks of the huge gas chambers and crematoria could be seen on the horizon ahead. Walking alone down that road, Doug became one of the victims who had stood on the Birkenau railway platform, condemned to death by Dr. Mengele. It was just that easy a sentence; one flick of the doctor's riding crop meant life or death.

The road Doug was walking on is notorious for the pits that stand on either side. Pits filled with remains of countless babies and small children. How many had been roughly grabbed from their parent's helpless arms? As he walked, Doug could hear babies crying with hunger and disease, two- and three-year-olds brutally tossed as so much garbage into the burning pits.

He stared at the tufts of grass now covering the pits; his mind ached, he was still hearing the little ones' terrified cries, he could smell burning flesh, his head reeled. "Oh Father, oh my Father," he cried as he walked. Grief had enveloped him. His heart broke, he sobbed, and tears fell into the dust at his feet.

Doug cried for the remaining Jews in Poland, the remaining Jews in all of Europe. He cried for their release to Israel. "My God, how blind people are. They must see that it could all happen again one day. The Book of Jeremiah even speaks about 'Jacob's Trouble.' Can't they hear the voices of the dead crying out?" In his despair, Doug made a vow on that road. "I will bear witness to them," he promised God.

From behind, a hand tapped him on the shoulder. The gentle hand turned Doug around to a kindly face, with inquiring eyes. The gray-haired gentleman was Austrian. "You are so young, so why do you weep, son?" he asked, trying to comfort Doug.

"The Lord has sent me to weep for His people," Doug explained.

The stranger listened; sorrow filled his face. He replied, "I lost seventeen of my family here."

"Have you ever been to Israel?" Doug looked up into the sad eyes.

"Not yet," came the awkward reply.

"Then don't delay." Doug's words were filled with conviction. Looking around, he continued, "How many planned to get out of Europe before the dam broke? Will you go to Israel? You must go!"

"Yes," the Austrian replied, "I will go."

"I believe in the sun even when it is not shining. I believe in love even when not feeling it. I believe in God even when He is silent." [4]

POLAND

From the Jerusalem Post, January 28th 1985

Eight Jewish twins return to Auschwitz 'as human beings'

OSWIECIM. Poland (AP). — Jewish twins used as laboratory test animals by Auschwitz's "Angel of Death." Dr. Josef Mengele, yesterday relived the horrors of the Nazi extermination centre as they returned here for the first time in 40 years to re-enact the forced "death march" before the camp's liberation.

As a steady snow fell, eight surviving Mengele twins — five from Israel and three from the U.S. — marched from the Birkenau extermination camp to Auschwitz along the route they followed on January 27, 1945.

"I thought it was a wonderful feeling to walk the same streets, because I had never walked them before as a free human being," said Eva Kor, 50, of the U.S., who walked with her twin sister, Miriam Zeiger, of Israel.

"Forty years ago I could never imagine that one day I would be singing Jewish songs in Auschwitz," Kor said.

As they marched along the three-kilometre route, the twins and several dozen friends and family members sang in Hebrew.

They wore yellow stars of David with inscriptions reading "Jude" and carried a banner in Hebrew and French reading "I accuse."

At Auschwitz they marched under the main gate to the camp that still bears the inscription in German that "work makes you free."

The mayor of Oswiecim, the town in southern Poland where the camp is situated, welcomed them at a brick barracks that is now a memorial dedicated to the six million Jews who perished in the Holocaust, 2.5 million of them at Auschwitz.

Many of the surviving twins cried as they stood on the railway ramp in the same spot where, surrounded by shouting SS men and barking dogs, they came face-to-face with Mengele, who sent their parents and grandparents, brothers and sisters, to the gas chamber and condemned them to cruel medical experiments.

On the railway ramp, the twins placed a wreath with a memorial plaque bearing the pledge, "We will not rest until Dr. Josef Mengele is caught and brought to justice."

The twins were spared from the gas chambers by Mengele for his pseudo-medical experiments in genetic engineering aimed at breeding a master Aryan race. Of 750 pairs of twins, only 180 children survived the ordeal.

The twins said they have decided to speak out about their experiences after years of silence in the hope it will lead to intensified efforts to capture Mengele, the most wanted Nazi war criminal still at large.

On yesterday's march with the twins were two Israeli Knesset members — Shevah Weiss (Labour) and Dov Shilansky (Herut), both Holocaust survivors.

The liberation of Auschwitz was also commemorated yesterday in West Berlin, where 800 people gathered in the Jewish

Community House to "honour the victims and condemn the perpetrators" and in Vienna, where delegates to the World Jewish Congress said *kaddish.*

In Moscow, the official news media have marked the date with praise for the Red Army troops who liberated the camp.

Jay Rawlings
Meridel Rawlings
BRAZIL

4

Brit Hadashah

It was Purim. We found the Rabbi at the Jewish school. He had been teaching the story of the Jews' survival from the Book of Esther. Later that afternoon at the synagogue, in the privacy of his study, Jay and I were able to explain our desire to speak with him of the importance of educating his people to go to Israel. Rabbi David very warmly received us and invited us to Shabbat service the following day.

I remember how disappointed I was at my first Shabbat service there. Upstairs in the balcony, mothers let their children run wild, chewing gum, eating cookies and throwing papers. The women appeared completely alienated from all that the men were involved in downstairs. Although they had dressed for the occasion and had come to service, the majority were busily engaged in local gossip. I was puzzled.

Later, the Rabbi explained that he was the first Rabbi this community had ever had. Everyone was making adjustments. He seemed to appreciate the fact that Jay and I sensed the delicate position in which he stood, wanting to bring his people into more traditional ways, and yet needing to win them slowly by not making too many radical changes all at once.

We were saying goodbye at the door of the synagogue when he asked, "Would you be free to come to a dinner next Wednesday evening? The Bnai Brith are going to officially welcome my family and me to the community," he explained.

"We would be delighted," Jay responded.

On the way home Jay said, "This Rabbi takes his Orthodoxy very seriously." "Why?" I asked. "Well, I noticed that he slept at the synagogue on Friday evening and remained there until Shabbat finished at sundown on Saturday. That's dedication," he replied with a smile.

Four days later everyone in the community turned out for the dinner, which proved to be a gala affair. Sumptuous dishes filled beautifully appointed tables covered with white linen. Afterward, the President of the community proposed a toast to Rabbi David and Raquel, his petite French wife. The audience rose in unison and responded by filling the banqueting room with applause.

Rabbi David began his speech slowly and shyly in the newly learned Portuguese language. He shared his hopes and aspirations for their future together in Brazil. Then, to our surprise, he said, "I have invited two friends of Israel here tonight. I want Jay to stand and share with you many of the things we have discussed in private. The only words that I find to describe this man and his wife are 'hassidic goyim.'" While laughing, I thought, "Why didn't he give us some advance notice?" Every eye in the room was on us.

Undaunted, Jay stood to his feet and began in Portuguese. "I want you all to know that this is a complete surprise to me, and I count it a great honor to be called upon by your Rabbi. I trust that you realize the Lord has made you wait a very long time for a Rabbi so that He could choose the best for you." Applause filled the room.

He continued, "I want us to think tonight for just a few moments about that strange vision that your prophet Ezekiel had, you know, the one of the dry bones."[1] A ripple of laughter threaded its way through the crowd.

"The Scripture says that those bones represent the whole

---

[1] Ezekiel 37.

house of Israel. Before his eyes, Ezekiel saw the bones come together with sinews and flesh; last of all, the Spirit of God entered into them and they rose up, an army of men. I believe God showed Ezekiel the Land of Israel as she would come to birth as a Jewish nation in 1948 after 2500 years. We all know that, today, Israel is a spiritual and political entity in the earth, and just as important, Israel is also an example to the rest of the world that God keeps His promises."

Jay spoke lovingly, looking directly into the faces of his attentive audience. "Then Ezekiel prophesied that God would open the graves of His people and bring them up to their own land. This mighty ingathering began in the late 1800's, and moved with great force in the 1940's and 1950's. Even today, Jews from every corner of the earth are still coming out of their graves. For example, Russia is a graveyard to her Jewish population, which is awakened and bitterly persecuted for their desire to return to Israel. Concerned believers world wide are fasting and praying for their release. Thousands of Christians around the world entered into a three day Esther fast at Passover, taking neither food nor water, specifically for the safety and release of Soviet Jewry. All over Europe today, they have made preparation to clothe and feed and shelter hundreds of thousands of Soviet Jews as they exodus from Russia. It will happen for Isaiah says:

"I WILL say to the north, Give up; and to the south, Keep not back; bring my sons from far, and my daughters from the ends of the earth".[2] Abraham was drawn to the land of promise because he believed the word of the Lord and followed on by faith. Exactly the same phenomenon is taking place among Abraham's seed today.

Ezekiel hints at this day when he says, "A new heart also will I give you, and a new spirit will I put within you: And I will put my spirit within you and cause you to walk in my

[2] Isaiah, 43:6.

statutes and ye shall keep mine ordinances and do them."[3] This dovetails with what Jeremiah said, "Behold the days come, saith the Lord, that I will make a new covenant with the house of Israel, and with the house of Judah. Not according to the covenant that I made with their fathers . . . for they shall ALL know me, from the least of them unto the greatest of them . . . for I WILL forgive their iniquity, and I WILL remember their sin no more."[4] This new covenant secures the personal revelation of the Lord to every believer. It assures the complete oblivion of sins. It is unconditional, final and irreversible. This promise is to every Jew, young and old, boy or girl. Remember, the new covenant depends upon the mercy of God, for He says repeatedly, "I WILL". I believe that in each one of us there is a hunger and thirst for the true reality only found when one comes back to the Father. We must seek and we *will* find. I have, and am greatly blessed as a result!

Afterward, Jay couldn't remember what he had said, but the words had flowed out of his soul and the people had responded. Everyone was on their feet, hands clapping. Women came to us, faces stained with mascara from tears. They hugged us tightly and demanded, "What was it we felt when you were speaking?"

"That was God letting you know by His Spirit that I was speaking the truth," Jay said. In no time, it seemed, our limousine was at the door, compliments of the community.

During our stay in this city, Rabbi David and Jay met together regularly to study the Bible. A bond of love developed as a result of their common desire for God and love for His people.

BRAZIL

---

[3] Ezekiel 36:26a, 27.

[4] Jeremiah 31:31, 32a.

Jay Rawlings
Meridel Rawlings
BRAZIL

5
Fishers and Hunters

The air was hot and sticky as we boarded the bus in Rio de Janeiro. Our destination was a cool alpine resort town. The road twisted and wound its way through landscapes similar to Switzerland. We saw magnificent weekend villas tucked in amongst the gently rolling hills and valleys. In contrast, jagged rock formations, thrust violently upward in past millennia, stood like tall accusing fingers.

Jessie was easily found upon arrival at our destination, for his hotel housed the only synagogue in town. As we entered, thick wooden doors swung into the receiving hall, where the aroma of chicken soup filled the air. Somehow it matched the red checkered tablecloths, polished wooden floors, and mounted deer's head in the dining room. Jessie was obviously a hard worker, a man of plain speech and simple taste.

"Shalom. We're looking for the Shul," I said, looking around.

Jay and I were startled by his abruptness. "Who scnt you?" was his first question. It wasn't a personal affront; he simply wanted to know.

"The Lord sent us, Jessie!" Jay said very matter of factly.

"Ah... ah, I see," said Jessie. Wondering what to do with us, he led us to the door of his synagogue. The late afternoon light made the already dingy room seem even darker. A faint musty smell permeated everything. Jay thumbed through a couple of the prayer books. Jessie broke through the silence with, "My family were the only ones to get out of Luxembourg before the war. My father was a religious man, a tailor by trade. He always said that I would be a Rabbi, and now I do what I can. The community here have saved money to build a new synagogue."

Instinctively, we felt that this simple little hotel owner was God's man hidden away in this sophisticated resort town. He drew back the curtains and very proudly displayed the Torah scrolls wrapped in velvet mantles. He lovingly caressed them with his hands roughened by hard work.

"Jessie, do you know that your people are in danger here?"

"Yes, I know. I am the seer of this community and I know who watches us."

"You must tell your people to go and live in Israel. It's safe there."

"We'll get out just before the trouble comes," he responded quickly.

"You must tell anyone who will listen...." Jay's voice had a serious quality. "Why wait?" He was interrupted.

"I know who you are," said Jessie, recognition shining in his eyes. "You are some of those fishers." Smiling, he surprised us by quoting:

> Behold, I will send for many fishers,
> saith the Lord, and they shall fish them.[1]

"Yes, Jessie," Jay warned, "we're surprised and delighted that you know who we are, but don't make the mistake of waiting too long, because you know the hunters will come afterward."

We accepted his kind invitation for coffee and apple strudle, but sadness seemed to surround us when we said goodbye to this newly found friend. He was one of the few we

---

[1] Jeremiah 16:16.

had met who understood perfectly what we were saying. We enjoyed the cool evening air, strolling through the pleasant streets back to the bus depot with just a five-minute wait before departure to Rio on the last bus. As the bus drove out of the little town, lights were blinking on in the twilight. We saw it as a charming little place of tree-lined avenues, European cuisine, bowling greens and tennis courts, riding stables and theaters, one very small synagogue and... hunters....

BRAZIL

6
Afghanistan Connection

Edward Hull was sitting in the Pan Am office in Washington, D.C., putting the finishing touches on an around-the-world tour for 15 people. Heavy lines traced their way across his brow, his hair was thin on top and gray at the temples; he was not as young as he used to be by any means. However, Ed felt as good as new! The savage, competitive life as a salesman was over. Heavy drinking, chain smoking and running around on his wife and family were scenes of a past that would never return. Not only was he leading Christian tours to the far-flung corners of the world now, he delighted in looking up the Jewish communities in every major city that he visited. The question just now was, should he bother stopping in Afghanistan or not; just a 12-hour layover—would it be worth it? "Are there any Jews there or not?" he mused.

"Yes, go ahead and book us," he said with decisiveness to the salesgirl. "It will be a Saturday morning—maybe we can find the synagogue," he thought hopefully.

Ed had prepared many of his tour members by taking them to observe synagogue worship in Washington, D.C., but first he had given them some instruction concerning the Jewish Sabbath. "The coming of the Shabbat is likened to a queen, when she enters," Ed explained. "In Jerusalem the streets are emptied, giving the city a deserted feeling. Barriers are placed across the roads, forbidding the entry of any vehicles. As the stars appear, you see people, old and young, strolling from synagogues. Peace has in fact come down upon the city, giving it an eternal quality that is so tangible you can almost touch it. In Jewish homes everywhere, the women have prepared the beautiful Shabbat meal, candles have been lit, men are home from the synagogues, loved ones are gathered together and the ritual of coming to the altar begins. In the Jewish home, the table is considered to be an altar. Shabbat begins on Friday evening, which is the end of the sixth day and the beginning of the seventh. 'Shabbat Shalom!' is the greeting you say, meaning 'Sabbath Peace!'"

Three weeks later Ed and the tour members visited a synagogue in downtown Washington. It was Rosh Ha-Shanah, the Jewish New Year. Ed spoke quietly in the vestibule, "Allow me to describe some of the ritual objects of worship you will see here, before we enter.

"The Torah scroll is the holiest and most important object in the synagogue. It is housed in the Ark and is taken out for public reading four times a week. The scroll itself is hand-written on parchment and must be exact in its wording. Covering the scrolls is a mantle through the top of which protrude the two staves called 'Trees of Life.' Over the front of the mantle is a breastplate or shield. Hung from the staves, it designates the portions to be read on various occasions such as the festivals. It is called a breastplate to recall that it was worn by the High Priest in the Temple. Inside the Ark a light is usually kept burning as a symbolic reminder of the candelabra menorah of the Temple and was originally placed in a niche in the western wall of the synagogue.

"One of the most important components of the synagogue service is the public reading of the Torah. The raised platform from which it is read is called the 'bimah' which is Hebrew for 'platform.'"

Three days later, the Pan Am carrier touched down on the tarmac near Kabul, Afghanistan. Weary Americans alighted into the clear crisp air. The early morning sun shone brilliantly upon the barren and dry landscape rimmed by rugged mountains in the distance. Dozens of military vehicles lined the runway. The red hammer and sickle stamped on their doors left no confusion as to their ownership. The atmosphere was heavy with a frightening sense of oppression. Soldiers filled the airport lobby. "They must be expecting trouble," thought Ed, an experienced traveller in Communist countries. However, he remained calm.

The local "guide" informed him, "You were booked into the Intercontinental Hotel, but it was damaged by rebels in the night. I will take you to a very comfortable guest house where you can rest. Your departure time is six p.m. this evening. I've arranged a guided tour for you...."

Ed broke in, "Thank you very much. We're pretty tired after our long flight and will rest now. May we tour this afternoon?"

"Yes, that will be fine," the guide smiled trying to please. Ed inquired in the passengers' lounge as to the layout of the city. "Say," he said casually to the information clerk, "can you give me directions to the local synagogue here?" The clerk simply looked on his map and scribbled the address down on a scrap of paper. "Thanks!" Ed stuffed the map and precious scrap of paper into his coat pocket.

By the time Ed and the tired Americans arrived at the door of the synagogue it was nine a.m. As they walked in, the place was instantly astir. "Friends from America!" There was a sense of delight in the whispers that sent the message from mouth to ear, mouth to ear, until the president of the community, who was standing at the bimah or podium of the synagogue, got the message. He paused for a second until all of the tour group were standing inside the doors.

"Let our guests come in," he called out cordially in perfect English.

A kindly, stooped gentleman led the men to empty places amongst the men, and the women were taken aside to a special area for women behind latticework at the very back of the synagogue. The service continued as if no interruption had taken place. Everyone stood and sang:

Shmah Israel	Hear O Israel
Adonai Elohenu	The Lord our God
Adonai Echad.	The Lord is One.

Ed had explained earlier that the name "Shmah Israel" was given to the prayer found in Deuteronomy 6:4. This Scripture is found written in every synagogue around the world. The last words that a Jew says if he is laying down his life as a martyr are, "Hear, O Israel, the Lord our God, the Lord is one."

Some Scriptures were read and the men sang others in unison. The oriental melodies were foreign-sounding to American ears. A little later the Torah scrolls were reverently rewrapped and returned to the Ark. The formal service was coming to a close.

Then the gentleman in charge said, "Let our guests come forward please. You have just come from America?" he queried, trying to conceal his pleasure.

"Yes," Ed responded with a big grin and hearty handshake. "We represent Christians who love Zion and pray for her peace. We have come especially this morning to bring you a word of encouragement and greetings from your communities in North and South America, South Africa and Australia. We bring you peace!"

Ed waited a few more seconds, gave the signal and the entire group broke into song, "Hevenu Shalom Alechem." In response, the men rose to their feet and everyone joined in singing the well-known Hebrew chorus.

"Please, Sir," said the president, "would you have some further word to speak to us?"

Ed waited until they were seated and began, "Gentlemen, do you know that the Holy One of Israel is pouring out His Spirit upon the nations of the earth in preparation for the coming of the Messiah? Goyim like myself are awakening to the truth that we must stand with Israel and with the Jews, for their preservation is also our preservation. You have given us all that is dearest to us in life—the Scriptures, family life, and Jesus." As he spoke, a peculiar sense of urgency filled his thinking. "Jews are also responding to the Ruach Ha-Kodesh because they are coming to Israel from the four corners of the earth— many with nothing, just the clothes on their backs. Have you seriously," and Ed said the word "seriously" very very slowly, "considered going home to Israel before the day comes when you will not be able to go? There your sons and grandsons will grow up a free and proud people." There was an uncomfortable strain in the air.

Ed's theme changed! Everyone was surprised when he looked out over the audience and said, "I would like to pray for you and the Lord your God will heal you!" His promise to your fathers was, 'I am the Lord that healeth thee,'[1] and in Psalm 107:20 it says, 'He sent His word, and healed them, and delivered them from their destructions.'"

Without a moment's hesitation, a small, bent form shuffled forward. "My name is Shmuel Esri and I have trouble with my eyes." He spoke English well.

After Ed's simple prayer on his behalf, Shmuel's eyes DID focus better! One by one, the men came forward in faith to receive prayer. Complaints such as high blood pressure, arthritis, heart trouble and deafness were healed as the covenant that God had given to His people was activated by the prayer of faith.

There was a lightness that came into the room, as indeed each man actually did feel better. Loud Amens and Baruch Ha-Shems expressed the joy welling up within them, joy that they hadn't experienced for many years.

Ed said, "I would like to leave you with this promise, 'If thou wilt diligently hearken to the voice of the Lord, thy God, and wilt do that which is right in His sight, and wilt give ear to

---

[1] Exodus 15:26.

His commandments, and keep all His statutes, I will put none of these diseases upon thee, . . . for I am the Lord that healeth thee.'"

The president rose to the occasion. "Come with me," he beckoned to Ed and led the way to the front of the sanctuary. There he ceremoniously took a small sidur or prayer book and laid it in his new friend's large gentle hands. Warmth and admiration were shining in the president's eyes as he looked up into the face of the most unusual non-Jew he had ever met. "Thank you for your visit from the outside world, especially in these times," he whispered.

AFGHANISTAN

Jay Rawlings
Meridel Rawlings
ARGENTINA

7
Stammering Lips

Argentina was seething. Jay had been to Buenos Aires twice before, sharing with the Israeli ambassador, rabbis and presidents in one of the world's largest Jewish communities. Yet, we both sensed an urgency to return and spend time in the city. Newspaper articles said that 15,000 individuals were missing. There was talk of firing squads and flights carrying heavily sedated prisoners out over the ocean, where they were thrown into the sea alive but unconscious. Tension filled the air. Everyone sensed it—grocers, housewives, children, business executives. In spite of the signs, very few leaders heeded our warnings, and continued to live in the volatile atmosphere.

A gentleman from the Jewish Agency introduced himself to us as Isaac Shamiyeh and asked if he might come and spend an evening with us. Isaac's coffee and peach shortcake sat untouched on the coffee table next to him. He had heard about our visit previously and wanted answers. Persistently he questioned our message to the Jewish community.

"Who gave you this information? How could you know these details? What are you basing your statements on?" he demanded quietly.

"You can investigate us," Jay smiled, "but you'll find nothing. We are a praying people and have given ourselves over to visiting the Jewish communities around the world. Isaac, we love your people," he added. "But I can certainly understand your concern," Jay paused. "What if we *were* leading your people astray?"

"No, that isn't what I'm concerned about," Isaac tried to assure us. "It's WHAT you are saying. How could you possibly understand the situation here, I mean in detail?"

"This may sound too simple for you," I broke in, just coming downstairs from putting the boys to sleep, "but it's true. We pray, and prayer is not only talking, it is also listening, hearing, seeing and understanding! Prayer puts us in touch with reality, the invisible first and then the visible or tangible, the here and now."

Jay picked up the theme, "You must also understand that we are a Bible-believing people and whatever we see, by dreams or visions, or hear in our ear, must be in line with the Scriptures. We believe the prophets have spoken about the day in which we live."

"Well," Isaac responded, "I believe that. My family came from Morocco, and visions and dreams were not strange to them." At the close of the evening he said, "I didn't mean to make you feel uncomfortable." He looked at us apologetically, "but you know, we had to be sure! Keep up the good work."

A week later, Jay was invited to address the board members of the Grand Temple downtown. The chairman spoke to his colleagues, "Gentlemen, I have called this meeting for I feel we should hear what these friends have to say."

Jay poured his heart out. He spelled out the impending dangers and encouraged each successful man seated around the table to sell his holdings and move to Israel. The message was certainly not a popular one. We were treated very kindly, but the majority carefully contradicted Jay, saying that all was well in Argentina. We soon felt as though our visit was fruitless, consequently disappointment filled our minds and hearts all the way home on the train.

A pleasant surprise came later: Rav Jacobs, a Conservative

Rabbi and recent immigrant from Eastern Europe, opened the doors of his modern synagogue to us. We counted it a privilege to be so cordially received. His congregation listened intently to our warning and applauded as Jay's discourse came to a close. Later, many drew their chairs into a circle for a session of questions and answers.

Rav Jacobs invited us to his home the following week. He explained that his scholarly wife, Leah, was a translator for a large publishing company, and that she spoke nine languages fluently. At the present she was translating a large volume entitled *The History of Pentecost.* "I have a few questions too," he smiled, "see you then."

Immediately upon our arrival, as Rabbi Jacobs was ushering us to a sofa, he asked Jay, "When I receive the experience of the Ruach Ha-Kodesh, will I speak in other tongues?"

"Well," Jay suggested, "the very best thing to do is to see what the prophet Isaiah had to say about it." The Rabbi slipped over to his prestigious collection of leather-bound volumes and brought out the Haftorahs.

"The Scripture we are looking for is Isaiah, Chapter 28, Verses 11 and 12," Jay volunteered.

The Rabbi eagerly turned the gilt-edged pages and quickly read in Hebrew first and then English:

> For with stammering lips and another tongue will He speak to this people. To whom He said, This is the rest wherewith ye may cause the weary to rest; and this is the refreshing: yet they would not hear.

He then looked up at Jay, waiting for his comments.

"Yes, you will find yourself speaking in not just one, but in many different languages, known and unknown, which you have never learned.[1] The purpose is to give you greater power

---

[1] Acts 2:3, 4.

and ability to communicate with the Lord in prayer. New strength will come to you first, and then to your people."

Leah served dinner and we spoke in detail of trouble coming not only to the Jews of Argentina, but to all of South America. Leah became visibly upset.

"I don't believe it!" Her voice quavered with emotion, and her eyes were full of hurt and anger. "How can you say such a thing? We have been through the Holocaust, most of my family were lost, we came here with NOTHING, and now you warn us as they did the community in Europe in the 1930's. I can't bear the thought of it!" Her voice rose, she didn't realize that she was shouting.

Rabbi Jacobs gently placed his hand on her forearm. "Listen darling, just listen. It's not going to happen to us personally again," he consoled her. "We have suffered too much already. They are right in warning us. Would to God our people would listen." His keen eyes saw the danger, his ears took in every word, and we sensed that he was allowing our warning to be planted deeply within his heart.

Both the Rabbi and Leah were very interested in hearing how we lived and travelled by faith, with two small children and a third on the way. The four of us enjoyed one another's company. We shared many stories of the wonderful ways in which the Lord had blessed our lives and the lives of others. Jay concluded the conversation by saying, "We are first partakers of the promise, 'I will bless them that bless thee.'[2] I am the first to admit that we have been blessed above measure, as we've given our lives to seek out and try to comfort and warn our Jewish brethren."

Before we knew it, it was 1:30 in the morning. It seemed as though hardly an hour had passed. Jay excused us for the lateness of the hour. Very casually the Rabbi said, "Oh, Jay, tell me one more thing."

---

[2] Genesis 12:3.

"What's that?" he replied. We were standing in the doorway with our coats on.

"Does anyone have to lay hands on me to receive the infilling of the Holy Spirit?" He sought the answer in childlike simplicity.

"No," Jay assured him, "for this experience is a visitation by the Spirit of God. I'm sure you've read the Scriptures in Acts, Chapter 2 in the book Leah is translating. No hands were laid on the 120 who received this blessing in the story of Pentecost."

The Rabbi's face beamed with pleasure and he gave Jay a loving pat on the shoulder.

"See you in Israel!" I reminded him.

"Shalom."

"Shalom, shalom."

We were pleased to learn that, two years later, Rabbi Jacobs and his family were the first of their congregation to leave Argentina.

ARGENTINA

Jay Rawlings
Meridel Rawlings
RUSSIA

8
Let My People Go

The light has not gone out in Russia.

Alli Ruzer, Refusnik,
Moscow, April 1983

U.S. Senator Henry Jackson spearheaded an amendment to a bill passed in Congress, opening trade relations between the U.S.A. and the U.S.S.R. for the first time on a major scale. This amendment stated that the bill could not be enacted until there was freedom of emigration for minority groups from the U.S.S.R., with specific reference to the Jewish community and their desire to emigrate to Israel and other nations.

A visit to Russia held particular interest for Jay and I for many reasons. We realized that if our Christian brothers and sisters were being persecuted under the various communist regimes around the world, then our Jewish brothers and sisters were undergoing the very same pressures of hatred and ignorance. Along with other concerned Christians we began to pray and speak out on their behalf!

In the early period of the Soviet Union, numerous synagogues and other prayer houses disappeared and the meeting of Jews, particularly of the younger generation, for organized prayer and Torah study became a hazardous enterprise. After World War II, and especially during the regime of Krushchev

(1957–1964), a disastrous reduction of the remaining number of synagogues took place—from over 400 to 60 or 65. Some of them, mainly in Moscow and other large cities, remained intact in order to serve as both showplaces for visitors from abroad and as centers for supervision of the remnants of Jewish traditional life by the secret police.[1]

Paradoxically, at the same time in the early 1960's while synagogues were being closed down en masse, thousands and later tens of thousands of Jewish youth, reawakened to Jewish national consciousness, chose the synagogues, their courtyards and surroundings to demonstrate their Jewish identity by singing and dancing on Simhat Torah and other biblical holidays. These spontaneous gatherings in and around the few remaining synagogues, which have sometimes been dispersed by the police, have since become a constant feature of Soviet Jewish life, followed closely by diplomatic and press observers from abroad.

Several months prior to our departure, while I was praying in the evening, a persistent thought came to mind: "Meridel, I will give you the Russian tongue if you believe Me. I want you to speak to certain of My people." Then I saw a picture form before my eyes, and I was walking over the heads of men in prison. I had no understanding of what I was seeing. Later I would grasp its meaning.

That November in New York, Jay and I joined a tour group to Russia, made up of concerned citizens from all over North America. A handful of us carried Hebrew study books with cassette tapes and Bibles. Some of the large middle-aged women had stuffed the Holy Scriptures into their corsets, and a few teenagers used their toques and other ingenious methods to conceal the priceless materials. We all knew one thing: these gifts were to go into Russia. It was only much later that we discovered what to do with them once inside the country.

---

[1] *The Synagogue (Popular Judaica Library),* pp. 40, 41.

Leningrad looked formidable from the window of a tour bus in November! We passed block after block of great stone buildings, magnificent cathedrals, and many curved bridges spanning the dark icy waters of the Neva Kirovsk River. Parks were empty as winter winds scattered dead brown leaves against carefully chiseled statues commemorating Russia's famous leaders and artists. The broad streets appeared devoid of people.

The Hermitage Museum, crammed with vast art treasures, perhaps more than could be found in all of Europe, lacked warmth. In spite of the opulent magnificence, there was something missing as our guide gave out the various facts and figures in a mechanical manner. Was it the absence of joy that we noticed in the faces of the Russian visitors, workers and schoolchildren? They were quickly paraded past rich oils depicting themes from the Bible. Many of the art treasures bore signatures of the world's greatest masters, men who had taken their inspiration and themes from the Holy Scriptures. "How ironic," I thought, "citizens here are forbidden to own a Bible, and yet they are permitted to file by grandiose murals of the Bible story painted in great detail from Genesis to Revelation."

"I wonder *what* their guides' explanations are?" I said to Jay.

"Oh, probably that these are superstitions of a dark, unenlightened, unscientific mind." He looked as glum as his words.

That first night in Russia held a rude awakening for all of us. Our tour leader was informed briskly that a bearded young man from New York, one of our tour members, was locked up in the Central Police Agency in downtown Leningrad. He had been caught passing out three small pieces of paper with these words written on them in Russian:

> For God so loved the world that He
> gave His only begotten Son, that who-

soever believeth in Him should not
perish, but have everlasting life.[2]

One of the three Russians to whom he had given the paper had immediately reported him to the police. He was picked up, put in the back of a police van and taken immediately to their headquarters for interrogation. Luckily he knew nothing of the Hebrew literature a few of us were carrying. Later the same evening, K.G.B. men interrogated each of us closely, as an artist drew sketches of specific individuals.

"Understand this very clearly," the interpreter warned, his eyes the color of steel, "if any of you gives out one more piece of this kind of literature, we will immediately escort you all to the nearest border."

The prisoner was set free around 11:00 p.m., quite sobered by the whole experience. He had learned his lesson.

Was it possible that our rooms would be searched while we were out for long hours at a time "touring"? We expected the worst. Just in case, those of us who carried Bibles and Hebrew literature gathered together in one room and whispered out a plan. There were two identical gray suitcases on the tour, one filled with the passports and many airline tickets. It would be the decoy. We filled the other identical one with Bibles and Hebrew literature. Instead of carrying the tickets around with us, the men would take turns carrying this 85-pound suitcase of literature. It would come with us on every bus, and through every museum, into every restaurant and concert, right under the noses of guards and tour leaders. Hopefully they would be none the wiser. It had to be carried as though it weighed a mere 20 pounds, so the men frequently spelled each other off. The suitcase was never out of someone's watchful eye. It was only when we got to Moscow several days later that we knew what to do with the contents.

---

[2] John 3:16.

Throughout the duration of our visit, Jay and I made a point of looking for the hidden microphones in our various bedrooms, often found behind the drapes or under window-sills. Every night before going to bed, we enjoyed reading choice portions of Scripture into them. One night during the reading we heard a "bump" at the door. Jay opened it, surprising three large Russian men dressed in suits kneeling on the floor listening.

"Yes, is there something that we can do for you?" my husband asked.

"Ah, er, excuse us, we have lost something," was their embarrassed excuse. They quickly retreated down the hall.

After this our telephone rang off and on. The voice of a young girl, speaking very familiarly in English, said, "Hello, Mrs. Rawlings. We understand you have Bibles for us Christians in the underground. Could I meet you in your hotel lobby with my Daddy?" She sounded so sweet and innocent.

"You are completely mistaken, my dear," my voice was firm and cool, "we have no Bibles." I hung up. We were determined not to be tricked.

Another night after dinner, we slipped out of the hotel and quickly faded into the shadows of the dark streets of Leningrad. Jay met a Cuban on the street, and in Spanish we were directed to a subway entrance and took the escalator hundreds of feet down to the trains. Magnificent crystal chandeliers lit up the interior of the waiting station! Richly illustrated murals depicted scenes from the Great Revolution. My fashionable red woolen coat drew a few glances. Was it anti-American sentiment I was sensing, or did my coat make the women envious, I wondered. How could we overcome the invisible barrier of culture, ideology and language that stood so firmly between us and the Russian people?

The train cars were almost empty, as the evening rush was over. We sat down beside a tired-looking man whose face was lined with wrinkles. He sat slouched over, staring blankly ahead. We rode for some time, and all of a sudden that small voice, that I have learned is the voice of the Lord, began to speak. "Speak now!" It was a command.

I jumped a little and my stomach seemed to turn over with fright. Instantaneously I recalled the promise of many months ago, when I was down on my knees the Lord said, "I will give you the Russian tongue." I had faith to believe it then, but now my mind was shouting silently, "Oh no, I can't, I can't!"

"NOW!" came the firm command. My heart was pounding and my hands were icy as I turned to speak to the stranger. As I opened my mouth in faith, a language of the Holy Spirit poured forth. I stopped, waiting. In utter amazement the bent head lifted and turned in my direction, his wrinkled face burst into a sunny smile and the stranger began to speak rapidly as if in answer to what I had said. He stopped, smiling very warmly.

I picked up the conversation, not understanding what I was saying. Words simply spilled out of my mouth, sounds that were foreign to my own ears seemed to create an amazing response in this stranger. I paused.

He began speaking immediately and became very excited, smiling at me through the tears that were rolling down his tired face. He paused, and waited. I continued on speaking, absolutely amazed by what was happening. A mantle of peace came down upon both of us as this supernaturally arranged and composed conversation was taking place. It was as though time stood still. This stranger spoke to me with familiarity and openness, as though I were a member of his own family. My red coat was no longer a point of separation; neither were my culture nor my beliefs. The subway car lurched and jolted to a very fast stop, the doors flew open and he indicated that he had to get off. Before leaving, he squeezed both of my hands and his face shone like an angel's. He looked so alive and delighted that the tired lines had almost disappeared. I wondered, still amazed, what precious things the Spirit of God had spoken to him even though I didn't understand a word. I sat very still for a long time, my knees had turned to water and my heart was still pounding.

I was trembling with the knowledge of what had just transpired. How great our God is, I marvelled, and silently worshipped Him right there! How worthy He is to be appreciated and praised. He alone breaks the bars and cruel bondages. He had melted our hearts by His great and wise heart of love. As I sat there I was reminded of the original miracle of speaking in tongues on the Day of Pentecost when the Holy Spirit spoke through Jews to Jews from many other nations in their own languages.[3] The Bible says they spoke of the wonderful works of God. Several times while in Russia, I was ordered to "SPEAK" by the Holy Spirit.

In Moscow we found the atmosphere much more oppressive than that of Leningrad. It was a city of gray buildings. Stores had very little to sell, and our enthusiasm evaporated when we saw older women, with bare hands, pushing brooms over the frozen streets. The temperature had dropped considerably, and the freezing November winter seemed to seep into our souls.

The suitcase of Bibles was getting heavier and heavier. The longer we stayed inside Russia the more we realized the seriousness of our intent. Need for God's wisdom forced the handful of us to pray until we got an answer of what to do with the literature. How unexpected it was when it came.

The Lord impressed us that we were to take these Bibles and Hebrew tapes and books to the Central Great Synagogue at Arkhispova Street in Moscow. He promised us His protection and His guidance. How could we do it, we wondered, as we were followed everywhere!

One afternoon was unscheduled, so we devised a plan. Three couples would get off our tour bus at the same place downtown. One would immediately catch a taxi and go to the Baptist Church to visit. The second would also catch a taxi

---

[3] Acts 2:6–11.

and go directly to the synagogue with the suitcase. And the third, Jay and I, would act as decoys and just walk the streets in the shopping area.

Characteristic of almost all the synagogues of the U.S.S.R. is the heavy atmosphere of fear of the secret police. It is generally believed that they listen to all conversations and keep a sharp observation of any contact between Soviet citizens and visitors from abroad.

Hurriedly, the couple carried the suitcase into the synagogue and asked to see Chief Rabbi Levine. The dear Rabbi was in. They were ushered into his office; the door was closed; little was said. The suitcase was laid on his desk and opened. When the Rabbi saw the treasure, he fell to his knees and kissed the hands of the couple who had brought him this gift. Tears coursed down his face in gratefulness. Quickly the suitcase was emptied. The couple left as speedily as they had come, carrying the gray suitcase with them.

You can imagine our relief and joy when we all arrived back at the hotel. The whole experience brought to mind Psalm 74:8, 19: "They said in their hearts, let us destroy them together. They have burned up all the synagogues of God in the land. O deliver not the soul of Thy turtledove unto the multitude of the wicked. Forget not the congregation of Thy poor for ever."

Our last evening in Russia was spent dining in an exclusive restaurant in Moscow. We shared a table with our young "Intourist" guide. During the course of the dinner, she announced proudly, "My father is a member of the Communist Party. Only 10% of the population carry this status and I'm a member of KOMOSOL, the Communist Youth Movement."

"My Father has a special place in His heart for all people—not just 10%. He is the great Creator, and He loves you and wants you to love Him," Jay gently replied while testing the caviar. She seemed to suffer his comment in silence, which was broken by a roar of engines carrying heavy military equipment past the restaurant. The chandeliers began to sway and the large panes of glass in the windows rattled. Several teenagers on the tour ran to the windows and many cried fearfully as they looked out and saw tanks and weapon-carriers rumble past. Our guide explained, "Tonight is the 55th Anniversary of the Bolshevik Revolution."

We all hurried over to the windows and stared out at the largest procession of military might any of us had ever seen. The very latest Soviet military power—tanks, missile-carriers and heavy guns—thundered past, shaking the frozen earth. I thought back to our first night in Russia, when one small verse from the Bible had caused such a stir! The god of this world in a great nation like Russia with all of her military force had been threatened by just one verse of Scripture.

Snow had begun to fall and it was cold that night as we walked briskly from the restaurant to Red Square. During the days of our visit, we crossed the length and breadth of it many times, praying specifically for the release of Soviet Jewry, and also for the multitudes of other persecuted peoples in Russia.

A personal letter that our tour leader composed had been sent to the Soviet leader, Leonid Brezhnev, stating that the Scriptures spoke specifically concerning the release of Jews from his nation. It stated, "The living God has commanded, 'I will say to the north, give up!'"[4]

The Kremlin's walls were dark and foreboding. I thought, "How ironic it is that today foreign dignitaries pass in and out of the Kremlin through a gate called Saviour's Gate." A moon partly hidden by clouds shone weakly down upon the golden onion domes of churches, now museums, within the Kremlin walls. Our guide had proudly pointed out the dozens of jewelled Bibles on display. The hands of a large clock pointed five minutes to midnight. It was late. I glanced over to Lenin's tomb with its solemn guards standing at attention. Seeing his corpse on display in an eerie red light had been a horrible experience. This was the man who wrote, "Every

[4] Isaiah 43:6a.

religious idea, every idea of God, even flirting with the idea of God, is unutterable vileness of the most dangerous kind, contagion of the most abominable kind. Millions of sins, filthy deeds, acts of violence and physical contagion are far less dangerous than the subtle, spiritual idea of God." He in turn had become a god to the people. However, in spite of party doctrine, throughout our stay in Russia many of us were under the distinct impression of being surrounded by multitudes of believers.

We walked past row upon row of the military hardware that we had seen and heard earlier as it rumbled by the restaurant, now on silent display in Red Square. The Spirit of Fear seemed to stalk the night, walking behind us, laughing and jeering at our prayers, telling us that our love and concern for Russia and her peoples were absolutely futile.

At five o'clock the next morning we were on the bus headed for the airport. The November wind was howling in the pre-dawn darkness, driving the snow on ahead of it. All of a sudden the driver jammed on his brakes. He threw the door of the bus open and our guide ran from the bus with her hand over her mouth. My husband and the tour leader followed her to see what was wrong. There in the isolation and pre-dawn darkness on the highway behind the bus, our Intourist guide only had one thing to say. "I'm not sick," she whispered, "please, please pray for me." Our words to her had not been futile after all.

Just days later, upon our arrival in Jerusalem, we read this headline in the Jerusalem Post: "To Satisfy World Opinion Soviets willing to free 300,000 Jews in next decade".

Looking back now, we know that from 1972 until 1982 approximately 300,000 Jews were released from Russia. Unfortunately thousands went to the West, and today those who wish to leave Russia for Israel are languishing without hope.

It was years later when we met former prisoner of Zion and lawyer, Avraham Shifrin in Jerusalem, that we understood that we had indeed walked over the heads of prisoners in Russia, for he said many of the detention cells are beneath railway stations and under the main squares of cities, as described in his book, "The First Guidebook to Prisons and Concentration Camps in the Soviet Union." Bantam Books, available at P.O.Box 32, Zikhron Ya'akov, Israel.

RUSSIA

Krista Barten
Julia Tooley
AUSTRIA, BELGIUM

9
Noshreem I

The *Jewish Chronicle* carried an article entitled "Yordim." Yordim means literally "those who go down," in direct contrast to "olim," which means "those who go up." In this instance, it referred to families of Russian Jews who found that the reality of living in Israel was not as sustaining as their dreams of it were. The article went on to explain that many families sat stranded in Vienna and also at another unnamed place in Belgium. No solution had been found for these disillusioned people, who waited for visas to other countries. This problem was an embarrassment to various Jewish agencies, who sought for a solution.

Krista Barten, an executive secretary to a large American firm in Vienna, picked the article out of the newspaper at work. She brought it home to share with Julia Tooley, the teenage daughter of New Zealand friends. Julia was spending several weeks with Krista, having just completed eight months of study in a Hebrew Ulpan in Jerusalem. Her fair hair, blue eyes and peaches-and-cream complexion, along with her soft English accent, made her as beautiful on the outside as she was within. Julia was just eighteen years of age, and had already had the honor of personally visiting eighteen rabbis in South Africa. One Rabbi for every year of her life. She loved the Jews. Krista knew that Julia would be interested in this article.

A group of Soviet Jews was expected to arrive the following day at the railway station. Krista and Julia thought they might get more information there. Early the following morning they waited on the platform, surrounded by Austrian guards armed with submachine guns, on the alert against Arab terrorists. When the train finally arrived, twenty-seven men, women and children, Jews from Soviet Georgia, got out. They looked like hard-working country people, their faces tanned and weather-beaten. Bright shawls draped the ladies' heads. An old man was blind and led by his wife, just as old, dressed all in black. Another old-timer had proudly pinned his war medals across his chest for all to see. Julia gave candy to the young children. Surrounded by armed guards, the newly arrived Russian Jews slowly filed out of the station. All of their material possessions were stuffed into rope-tied suitcases or boxes. It was like a reenactment of the Exodus. The scene before her eyes caused a Scripture to pop into Julia's mind: "But the Lord liveth, which brought up and which led the seed of the house of Israel out of the north country, and from all countries whither I had driven them; and they shall dwell in their own land."[1]

"I hope they *all* stay in Israel," she thought.

Krista and Julia tried to get some information from the welcoming committee as to the whereabouts of the Yordim. One official looked up in exasperation and said, "Talk to the 'Caritas' people." "Caritas?" Krista repeated the clue and said, "Julia, that name was in the newspaper article. Let's see what we can find out."

Five days later, after driving from Vienna to Brussels, Krista and Julia stood before the secretary of a Catholic organization called "Caritas." Both young women eyed the secretary, their two passports open on her desk. "I'm looking for a friend," explained Krista on behalf of Julia, "a Russian student who was with my friend, Miss Tooley, in the Ulpan in

---

[1] Jeremiah 23:8.

Jerusalem. I understand that you can help us find where she might be located."

The secretary had been told not to give out any information, and all that she would finally offer was the name of the town on the northern seacoast where some of these Russians were housed.

That was enough. Delighted with this little piece of information, immediately Krista and Julia set out toward the northern coast and arrived at their destination by noon the following day. When they found the institution, it reminded them of a geriatric hospital, with only a ground floor constructed of drab gray stone. The lawns and gardens were well cared for. An uneasy quietness surrounded the place. The wire fences and guarded gate added to the mystery. Security police, whose responsibility was to shield the people from the press, eyed the two women suspiciously.

Approaching the guardhouse, Julia smiled and said, "I have come to see a friend; we went to Ulpan together in Jerusalem."

"We must look harmless," she thought, for the guard relaxed and opened the gate. Together Krista and Julia walked past all security into the building. Opening the door, they entered a large recreation room. "I must confess," whispered Krista, "this reminds me of the movies I've watched with heavy scenes in psychiatric hospitals."

Few women or children were present among the many men. The room was thick with cigarette smoke. Several men were pacing back and forth, shuffling their feet in an agitated and worried manner. They only nodded to other fellow-pacers as they shuffled past one another. Other men were playing cards, checkers or ping pong, while others were reading or chatting. They were obviously bored.

Julia communicated in Hebrew and English. The young men were strong in their hopes to go to Canada or America. "I've tried Israel," said a young fellow from Kiev, "but the good life is in the West. Yes, they were good to us in Israel, but we only had a little money, and economically Israel is having difficulties. It's hard to manage with such high inflation, and I don't want to go into the army." No one had any very strong arguments against Israel. It's just that the material richness of the West had gripped them, and minds were made up. "Once we make some money, we can always go back to Israel," the spokesman chided. "We have already made application for visas to the West," he informed the two women.

"We have an expression in English," Julia stood her ground, not offended by his roughness. "The grass looks greener on the other side of the fence."

The circle of listeners around the women began to grow as they explained to the men that their action of leaving Israel was absolutely contrary to the words of the Prophets. The older wage earners gave particular heed. One such man excused himself only to return with the Tanach. Before opening it, he ceremoniously put a kipah on his head. Then he offered the book to Julia. She leafed through it and pointed to the following verse in Ezekiel:

> For I will take you from among the heathen,
> and gather you out of all countries
> and will bring you into your own land.
> A new heart also will I give you, and
> a new spirit will I put within you.[2]

"You see, God wants to make every provision for you," she said. "Read all of this chapter. He promises blessing for those who make the land their home. Look," the men behind her followed her finger as it moved slowly down the page, "read what He promises." The Russian with the kipah read in Russian:

> I will increase them with men like a
> flock. As the holy flock... of Jerusalem

[2] Ezekiel 36:24, 26.

> in her solemn feasts; so shall the
> waste cities be filled with flocks
> of men: and they shall know that I
> am the Lord.[3]

Everyone stared hard at the book and then blinked at the two women. The Word of God was piercing through all of their intellectual and emotional arguments. They felt the truth of those words. God would give them an open door to His blessing by return.

"This is the visa to a good life," Julia pleaded, pointing to the Scriptures. One could feel that every man in the room had understood the message, for the pacing had stopped. The ping pong table stood silent. In their hearts, the Russians wanted the blessing. Quietly the girls shook the hands that were extended to them and then left.

As they approached the gate, the guard asked, "Did you find your friend?"

"No," Julia grinned, "but I found many others."

AUSTRIA
BELGIUM

[3] Ezekiel 36:37, 38.

Julia Tooley
AUSTRIA

10
Noshreem II

Spurred on by the success of finding the Yordim in northern Belgium, Julia went from one office to another in Vienna trying to discover the location of the second group of Yordim that she and Krista had read about. People seemed embarrassed by her inquiries. She had lots of determination and prayed for guidance.

One Sabbath, outside the large synagogue in Vienna several Jews paused to chat with each other. Julia heard German, Yiddish and Russian. A handful were recent Soviet arrivals, she guessed. She restrained herself from going over to ask if they knew where the Yordim were, and while she stood there wondering just what to do, a vision of dozens of different kinds of Jews filled her mind — an old Yemenite, a sophisticated Bostonian, a Hassid from New York, Jews from Russia, Kurdistan, India, Hong Kong — faces of Jews from all over the world came before her eyes. Then the still, small voice whispered into her ear, "You must not pray for one type of Jew to return, but you must pray for every Jew to return." Peace flooded Julia's heart as the concern and anxiety left. Somehow the Lord would help her find the Yordin in Vienna; she was on the right track!

Needing more time to think she paused to sit on a park bench opposite a statue of Strauss. "Can't You give me any more clues, Lord?" she entreated. Then in direct response to her prayer, before her eyes appeared a very ugly old building. She was careful to notice the detail in the vision. Several windows appeared to be broken, the drainpipes were sagging, shingles were missing from the roof — it was in a terrible state of disrepair. She thought as she saw the vision "It is either a jail or a concentration camp." She understood why she had seen the first vision in the courtyard of the synagogue, but she didn't completely understand why she had seen the second until a few weeks later.

Julia literally began to walk the city. After several days of walking and praying, one cold afternoon when she felt like quitting she heard the word, "STOP!" Julia stood still on the sidewalk and looked up. The Lord spoke again, "They are in that building." There, to her left, stood the very building she had seen by vision several days previously. She made a mental note of the general state of disrepair; drainpipes, roof and windows were just as she had seen.

Her heart was pounding with excitement as she approached the door. She knocked and knocked again, countless times. No one answered the door. She walked away bitterly disappointed, for she knew the people she sought were inside that building.

Julia returned the following day, and the next, and the next, each time knocking at the door until her knuckles ached. Men and women would look out of the windows at her, but would not come down to open the door. It was a strange and frustrating situation.

There was only one solution — fasting and prayer! Again Julia took her requests to God. "Show me how I can get into that building," she cried. "I've got to talk to those people, Lord. You told me to!" She waited in her room for the answer to come, and one day it came, "Go today and they will open the door." That still small voice had never failed to speak the truth.

She reached the building and stood breathless. Rosy cheeks and windblown hair only served to enhance her natural beauty. Joy danced in Julia's eyes as she climbed the steps to the closed door that she had longed to pass through for weeks. A young Russian Jew stood waiting on the top step.

"Hello," he said admiringly.

"I've come to visit today." Julia smiled. He immediately offered to introduce her to everyone in the building. That day, Julia visited the Russians whose faces she had seen peering out of the windows. In fact, she visited the entire building, room by room, family by family. Her presence was as a burst of sunshine through very gray clouds. Many of the young men teased her about her modest ways of dress, speech and conduct, but showed their approval by proposing marriage. Fearful, hurting, women welcomed her as a friend, for she conversed in Hebrew while dandling their babies on her knees. "Yes, I will return," she promised, and they responded by agreeing that the door would be open for her.

As soon as Julia left the building that first day, she went immediately to the Central Jewish Agency. She burst through the door, eyes aglow, cheeks aflame from the cold winter air. "I've found the Russians," she reported triumphantly.

"We knew where they were all the time," admitted the head of the Agency, appearing embarrassed. "You may have found them, but it won't do any good."

"Oh, yes it will!" she contradicted. "God told me that if I spoke to them, He would cause them to return to Israel." She hurried out of the office to tell her good news to others who would appreciate the miracle God had given to her that day.

Julia returned for many such visits; friendships blossomed and grew. Then she began to instruct them as to why they must return to Israel. "First of all," she explained, "the Lord said that He would gather you from the north country. Let's read it." She pointed to the most mischievous fellow in the circle of listeners to read the promise:

> But the Lord liveth that brought up the children of Israel from the land of the north, and from all the

> lands whither He had driven them: and I will bring them again into their land that I gave unto their fathers.[1]

"What nation in the world today is known as the north country?"

Recognition began to dawn upon faces of old and young alike. "Russia," was the unanimous answer. "Correct" said Julia excitedly, now read:

> Therefore the redeemed of the Lord shall return, and come with singing unto Zion; and everlasting joy shall be upon their head. They shall obtain gladness and joy; and sorrow and mourning shall flee away. I, even I, am He that comforteth you.[2]

"See, He says that He will meet you, He will comfort you, He will make the difference." Then she began to sing her favorite song:

> For ye shall go out with joy,
> and be led forth with peace:
> the mountains and the hills
> shall break forth into singing,
> And all the trees of the field
> shall clap their hands.[3]

She taught them the tune, and soon they all joined in using the Book of Isaiah as a songbook. When they finished the song, it was time for Julia to say her final goodbyes. She had dreaded this moment. Her eyes filled and tears spilled over, coursing down her young concerned face. The tears spoke to hearts as much as her words. "Remember, God's word cannot return unto Him void.[4] I'll look for you all in Israel." Quickly

---

[1] Jeremiah 16: 15.
[2] Isaiah 51: 11, 12.
[3] Isaiah 55: 12.
[4] Isaiah 55: 11.

she turned on her heel, flew down the stairs, and out the door into the street. The Yordim, old and young alike, crowded to the windows and waved to Julia; she waved back.

Two weeks after Julia left Vienna, Krista spied a small article in the *International Herald Tribune.* How delighted she was to read that the first group of Russian Yordim from Vienna had returned to Israel. She sat down and immediately wrote to Julia, who, upon receiving the good news in New Zealand, got up and danced for joy — once again God's word had proven to be true.

AUSTRIA

Author's Note:

Julia's life, from the age of 17 to 19, was spent encouraging Jews to immigrate to Israel. At the age of 20 she was killed in an automobile accident. The tragedy is partially dissolved, knowing that Julia had pleased her Lord by comforting His brethren.

Vee Gardner
BRAZIL

11
The Gentile Shaliach

What shall one then answer the messengers of the nations? That the Lord hath founded Zion, and the poor of His people shall trust in it.[1]

São Paulo, a bustling city of nine million, has one of the most active Jewish communities in South America. Vee Gardner's interview was scheduled for 9:30 Tuesday morning downtown in the Yiddish newspaper office.

Widowed at a young age, Vee found consolation in pouring her energies into visiting Jewish communities, and also sharing her concern for the Jewish people with many Christian communities. It was a pleasant change from the social responsibilities of a Philadelphia lawyer's widow. Her visits had brought a sense of purpose to an otherwise very lonely existence.

Vee stepped out of the elevator immaculately dressed, her large brown chignon accenting delicately clear features.

"Good morning. Are you the lady that made an appointment for an interview?" asked Mario, who had obviously been waiting for her.

"Yes, I am," she replied, smiling warmly.

"Please come this way."

---

[1] Isaiah: 14: 32.

He was a busy reporter looking for a story, and he didn't really think this woman would have too much vital information to offer. They entered his office and he closed the door. Switching on the tape recorder, he began impersonally.

"First of all, you said that you were a Christian. What sect are you?"

"Well," Vee began, "we are not a sect, but we are 'born-again' believers in Jesus. Our faith has come from a personal encounter with Him, which has resulted in a change of attitudes and even life styles."

"So what has this got to do with us Jews?"

"Well," she replied, "we represent a large body of Christians all over the world who love Israel and the Jewish people, but are not interested in proselytizing them. I am one of many who have been termed the 'Hassidim among the non-Jews'. We ALL know," she continued, "of the Christians termed 'righteous Gentiles' who protected Jews in various ways during the Holocaust. Many of them were born-again believers. Today the Ruach Ha-Kodesh, the Holy Spirit, is working in the earth creating a people who will avail their money, time and effort to stand up for Israel's right to exist." She changed the subject slightly and said, "As you know, many of your people are not safe; we both know what is happening in Argentina."

Vee's words made sense to Mario, who nodded in agreement. Intrigued by her sincerity he asked, "When did your interest in Israel begin?"

"In 1971, after much prayer, a group of us went to Russia to fast and pray for the release of Soviet Jews. According to the Scriptures, the Jewish exodus from Russia in the end-time will eclipse the great Jewish exodus from ancient Egypt. Jeremiah 16: 14 and 15 says:

> Therefore, behold the days come, saith the Lord, that it shall no more be said, the Lord liveth that brought up the children of Israel out of the land of

> Egypt, but the Lord liveth that brought up the children of Israel from the land of the north and from *all* the lands whither He had driven them; and I will bring them again into their land that I gave unto their fathers.

"From this Scripture," she continued, "we see that the return of the Jews from the north will parallel also a great return from all the other nations of the Diaspora. Incidentally, in the atlas, Moscow is directly north of Jerusalem."

"How have you been received so far?" he asked with interest.

Vee's face radiated with enthusiasm at Mario's new spark of interest. "Wonderfully well; in fact, a leader of the Jewish community in Ecuador told us after we went to warn them to leave, that the Israeli government had just sent a man to tell them the very same thing. He was shaken, but the other leaders of the community were not moved to further action. Jewish community leaders listen and document the purpose of our visit at length in their Hebrew and Yiddish papers. But that is not enough. Jeremiah tells us why." Vee quoted the following from Jeremiah 16: 16b which says:

> And after will I send for many hunters, and they shall hunt them from every mountain, and from every hill, and out of the holes of the rocks.

"Do you realize that the fierce hunters who hate the Jews are now overtaking the gentle fishers who love them?"

"I've never heard that before," said Mario, now sincerely interested.

Vee continued. "In 1974 we sensed there was great persecution coming to the Jews of Argentina. One year later, in *The Jerusalem Post*, Arye Dulzin, chairman of the Jewish Agency, wrote these headlines over his column on Argentine Jewry: 'They are in grave danger, but don't wish to be saved.' That was more than two years after they had been visited for the first time. Also in August 1976, there appeared this article in the *New York Times*, again on the Argentine community." She opened her leather bag and handed Mario a clipping from the *New York Times*, August 1976, entitled "Group in Argentina Vows War on Jews."

As Mario finished reading the article, he looked up and Vee spoke forcefully, "God sent us to the Zionist leaders and other heads of the Jewish community in Johannesburg, South Africa. We were warmly received, but again no action was taken to alert the South African Jews that danger for them was at hand. Ten months later we went again to warn them in the strongest terms to prepare to leave for Israel.

"As we sat with them, bloody riots were only eight miles away, labor strikes were on the increase and a tight government check on taking money, gold and diamonds out of the country had been put into force.

"They told us that they could not feel any imminent danger. We could hardly believe it." She continued speaking quickly, "Thank goodness two-thirds of the community in Zimbabwe have left, but what assurance of safety do the remaining Jews there have under a Marxist government?

"In French universities, atrocious anti-Jewish posters are upon the walls. In England, swastikas are found on Jewish gravestones. Here in North and South America, you read daily of the activities of the Neo-Nazi Movement."

Mario just sat back and let her talk. "I'll get a good story out of this," he thought to himself.

"The Jewish community in Beirut, Lebanon, could not have conceived of the destruction and tragedy that was about to befall their luxurious city, but the smoke still rises from its ruins and bodies lie unburied for days. Two hundred Jewish families fled years ago for their lives, leaving all behind." Vee paused to take a breath and continued, "Who really knows how many tens of thousands of Lebanese have been slaughtered by Syrian and PLO forces, while the nations have not raised a hand to help?"

"Oh," broke in Mario, "but Israel is the agressor now, according to world opinion."

"Lets face it," Vee expounded, the media is blatantly anti-Israel, no matter what Israel does."

"There is new danger facing the Jewish people today," Vee drew a deep breath. "The U.N. resolution equating Zionism with racism ushered in a new era of ideological, political and propaganda warfare against Zionism. Anti-Semitism is hatred of the Jews. Anti-Zionism is discrimination against Jews insofar as they define themselves as a people and as a nation. Do you realize that the Soviet Union, the Arab World and the Third World are unified into an international front because of anti-Zionism? This front seeks to destroy the Zionist model of freedom and independence, which could serve as a model for subjugated peoples everywhere.

"Anti-Zionism undermines the legitimacy of the State of Israel. If Zionism is so negative a phenomenon that it has been condemned by practically the entire world, the logical conclusion must be 'why should Israel continue to exist?'

"Parallels are becoming visible between the function of anti-Semitism in the 1930's and the role for which anti-Zionism is being used today. It is easier to fight anti-Semitism, which has been declared illegitimate. Anti-Zionism is more difficult because anti-Zionist activities are accepted as legitimate.

"The Lebanese war has cost Israel dearly in every way. Perhaps Mr. Arafat will be remembered as the man capable of bringing the Israeli army to a standstill. Meanwhile the world hears nothing of the anarchy and terror the PLO inflicted upon Lebanon. Take for example, the young girls who are forced at gun point to PLO dens where they were repeatedly raped, or the men who were crucified in Tyre!"

"What more is there to say?" She looked at Mario and shrugged her shoulders. "We continue to do all we can to awaken world Jewry to return to Israel before it is too late. The Argentine situation is one small example of what will befall Jewry in every nation of the Diaspora. God's promise of safety and spiritual renewal for you is in Eretz Israel."

Mario was speechless. "This *is* going to make interesting reading," he declared as he switched off the recorder. "Do you have a little more time?" he looked appreciatively at Vee.

"Surely," she replied.

He then called in other staff members to hear her startling message.

BRAZIL

Jay Rawlings
Meridel Rawlings
SOUTH AFRICA

12
Warnings

It was a blustery winter's day in South Africa. The Rabbi's plush office was upstairs in the very large synagogue. A gigantic man, the Rabbi stood six foot, six inches. His glasses were thick, and he wheezed and puffed on the cigarette that dangled from the corner of his mouth.

"What do you want?" his gruff voice demanded. Jay and I stood dwarfed in front of him. That comment and his size were enough to throw one off balance.

"Well, we've come to tell your people that it's time now to go home. We want you all to be a part of the blessing." Jay spoke with confidence.

The Rabbi continued to puff and wheeze, unmoved. After some minutes, we thought it time to excuse ourselves and turned to leave.

"Wait a minute," the Rabbi lifted his hand, motioning us to stop. Jay and I stood still. He said nothing but got up and went to the office next door. In a few minutes he returned with his hands on his hips and said, "We are having a board meeting today and want to arrange a time for you to speak to all of the community here." For the first time he broke into a broad smile! "Could you come over to my home tonight and we'll discuss it further?" Delighted, Jay accepted immediately.

That evening, we were royally received into the Rabbi's

home. His pert little wife, Rina, led us into the living room, where her husband sat in his favorite chair under a cloud of cigar smoke, wheezing and puffing. "Come in, come in. Sit down," he called. They both made us feel right at home.

"I've invited the President of the Jewish Board of Deputies over to meet you," the Rabbi made the introduction from his chair. The President, a slight man with bowed legs, wore a leg brace, for he had great difficulty in walking. His snow-white hair was parted in the middle, his intelligent blue eyes glistened, and his smile was sweet. He could hardly wait for us to be seated before his questions began.

"What do you think the future of Israel is? Do you foresee war — like Armageddon?"

"Yes," Jay was very direct, "according to the Bible, Ezekiel, Chapters 37 and 38 describe a devastating war."

"Well then," broke in the President, "do you think that it is right for you to go around telling people to go back to Israel?"

"Yes, I know it is the right thing to do because, although it may seem paradoxical, Israel is the land of promise to the Jews. It is the safest place for them in all the world. We believe the prophets teach that it is the Jew's responsibility to place himself in Israel at the mercy of God, if you will. It seems so hard to make the transition in the natural, but God knows the blessings you will reap in the long run. He has promised to meet His people there! We all know that anti-Semitism and now anti-Zionism is rising up around the world trying to suffocate the Jews in every nation."

"You know," broke in the Chief Rabbi, still puffing on his cigar, "that in the 1930's the Jews of Europe, and Germany particularly, were warned of the trouble ahead. A man named Jabotinsky went all over Europe and spoke to large audiences, telling them to leave before trouble came, but how many listened?"

"Don't we all wish they had," Jay agreed.

Everyone in the room nodded the affirmative.

"Tell me," the Rabbi continued, "why are you so interested in Israel?"

"We believe Israel is the apple of God's eye," I shared. "The Bible says so! All other nations move according to the prophetic word as it is being fulfilled in Israel. The Messiah will come to rule the earth, and Israel will be the land He rules from. She and her peoples will mirror the perfect mercy and justice of God Himself. Israel is the land of the future, and what a future awaits her. We've made our own personal aliyah and live in Jerusalem with our three boys."

Jay added, "Our families have asked us if we aren't afraid to live in Jerusalem. Our reply is, 'We would be afraid NOT to live there, because the Lord told us to make Jerusalem our home.' The Bible says 'neither shall the covenant of My peace be removed.'"[1]

"Who sent you?" the President queried. He paused a moment and answered his own question. "The Lord?"

Jay nodded the affirmative. "Yes, the Lord! Actually we have done a considerable amount of public relations work for Israel through our travels, films, paintings, T.V. interviews and writings."

The Rabbi began to speak again, and soon was almost preaching a sermon on why Jews should be back in Israel. He laid his cigar aside as he became more and more excited by the truth of his own words. "Jewish people will never be wiped off the face of the earth. Israel was never a viable nation under the Muslims, Turks or British; not until the Jews began to return from all over the world did the miracle happen. In 1968 we saw the beginnings of the great miracle of return of Russian Jewry. Those who had lived all their lives and had never known religious freedom, now desired it. Yes, yes, the miracle of Israel."

The room became quiet as conversation subsided.

---

[1] Isaiah 54: 10.

The Rabbi turned his attention to the musical instrument Jay had brought. "Come and sing," he invited, changing the subject completely.

Jay began to strum the auto-harp and sing a song written by one of Israel's favorite song writers. Just at that moment, Rina had the maid bring in a large cart of tea and cakes. He sang....

Lu yehi .... Let us pray

Chorus

Lu yehi, lu yehi, ana lu yehi
Kol sh'nevakesh lu yehi,
Lu yehi, lu yehi, ana lu yehi,
Kol sh'nevakesh lu yehi.

Let us pray, let us hope and believe, O Lord
Let us pray, let us hope and believe, O Lord
Let us pray and hope and believe
Let us pray and hope and believe

Verses:

Beyond the clouds upon the ocean
There's a white and lonely sail
Let us pray and hope and believe
I lit a candle at my window
And it's flame is shy and frail
Let us pray and hope and believe.

Rina, the Rabbi's wife, settled down into a soft chair, took off her shoes and put her feet up. She began swaying to the music and snapping her fingers to the lilt of the melody.

I hear a sound of drums and trumpets
From a battle not yet won
Let us pray and hope and believe
Although I know a thousand prayers
In my heart there's only one
Let us pray and hope and believe.

On the other side of the room, the Rabbi eyed the tea getting cold. He cleared his throat, and in a stage whisper to his wife said, "Tea is getting cold!"

"Lu yehi," she was singing the chorus along with Jay, but stopped to say, "Oh, it's so romantic; please sing the last verse." Jay sang on, with everyone in the room listening.

Afloating high above my country
There's an eagle and a dove
Let us pray and hope and believe.
A fading road — a dying summer
Keep your eye on those we love
Let us pray and hope and believe.
A little star at last is rising
It shall win the endless night
Let us pray ....
So let us pray and let us hope
And let us live to see its light.
Let us pray, let us hope and believe, O Lord
Let us pray and hope and believe.

When Jay came to the end of the song for the second time, the Rabbi leaned over to his friend, the President, and exclaimed for all to hear: "We ought to hire him as our cantor! *Now*, Rina," he mocked severely, "serve the tea." We all laughed.

Rina struggled to her feet and served everyone a sumptuous tea.

Later in the evening, as we were excusing ourselves, the Rabbi put a huge kindly hand on Jay's shoulder. "Now son — remember, you're to speak to our congregation this coming Saturday night and I want you to know that you and your wife are welcome in our home any time."

Rina walked us to the door and shared, "My father was

a Polish Rabbi and longed for Israel. You remind me of him. He was buried with a little satchel of soil from Israel under his head. He instilled a love for the land in me when I was just a child. God knows I've never lost my faith in Him, and I want you to know that tonight has renewed my faith in humanity."

SOUTH AFRICA

13
The Last Generation

On Shabbat afternoon Gidi, an Israeli working in the Consulate in Sydney, Australia, introduced Jay to a group of Jewish university students. They belonged to the Zionist youth movement called "Habonim," which means "the Builders." They met in a modest Australian home on a quiet, tree-lined street. After their business had been discussed, Jay was asked to speak on the future of Israel according to Bible prophecy.

Jay stood facing a room filled with young men, alive with interest. He began, "We all know Israel is of immense importance to the Lord. He has promised that she would be 'the head and not the tail'[1] among the nations of the earth. Today we can see the deserts blooming, trees stretching forth their branches upon once barren mountain slopes, and her people regathered from the four corners of the earth, carrying on their daily business, speaking the revived Biblical language of Hebrew. This has all taken place just as the prophets said that it would. Nowadays, we are seeing that Israel is becoming increasingly more of a focal point in world events. Great nations of the earth are trying to steer her into what is termed 'peace negotiations.' According to the prophets, there will be

---

[1] Deuteronomy 28: 13.

no lasting peace until the Messiah comes. Peace is as supernatural as the breath of life itself. Isaiah said that the ambassadors of peace shall weep bitterly. Israel may have a temporary type of peace, meaning an absence of war, with various of her Arab neighbors, but she will never have real peace with Muslim or Communist doctrines."

"Excuse me, Mr. Rawlings," a young man stood to his feet. "I think that what you are saying is unrealistic! You make it sound as though peace is an impossibility."

"Well, it depends on your definition of the word 'peace,'" Jay explained. "Has Israel had peace since her birth on May 14, 1948? You, of course, know the precautions that are taken to patrol schools and neighborhoods, etc. Terrorist bombs continue to snatch away the lives of innocent citizens, Jew, Muslim and Christian alike, homes are built with air raid shelters. I think you understand the point I am making here."

Many disagreed with what he had said, and a din of argument arose. Another student stood up and raised his hands.

"Shh. Let's at least hear what he has to say."

"Listen fellas, I will not argue." Jay was firm. "If you want to listen, good. If not, we can wrap it up right now!" An embarrassed silence ensued.

Jay continued, "We all know that a glorious golden age has been prophesied for Israel. She will become the capital of the world and nations will flow into her, the Scriptures say. The Messiah will rule, armaments will be converted to farm implements, and nation shall not lift up sword against nation, neither shall they learn war any more.[2] The Messiah will be called 'the Mighty God, the Everlasting Father, the Prince of Peace.'[3] Jeremiah described Him as 'Jehovah-Tsidkenu, the Lord our Righteousness.'[4] The prophets speak of the divine

---

[2] Micah 4: 3.

[3] Isaiah 9: 6.

[4] Jeremiah 23: 6.

nature of the Messiah. This coming King will rule with God's authority from the natural throne of David. He will be a descendant of King David and His birthplace was foretold as Bethlehem-Ephratah.[5] Daniel saw the Messiah as the Son of Man, standing, receiving dominion and glory and a kingdom in which all people, nations and languages would serve Him. Daniel received this vision from the Ancient of Days.[6]

Today, we are living in a very troubled world. The prophet Jeremiah saw a time of great trouble coming and called it 'Jacob's trouble.'[7] The archangel Michael came to Daniel, and you can read about this encounter in the Book of Daniel, Chapters 9 and 10:

> And after three score and two weeks
> shall Messiah be cut off
> but not for himself,
> and the people of the prince that
> shall come shall destroy the city
> and the sanctuary.[8]

> Now I am come to make thee understand
> what shall befall thy people
> in the latter days.[9]

"I think today the important thing for us to notice is that there are two princes that Daniel saw. One was the Messiah and the other was a false messiah. Scriptures in the New Testament teach that a man shall arise, deceiving many through his high-sounding words and through what will be called miraculous powers; this man shall become a political world ruler, claiming to have brought world peace. He will

[5] Micah 5:2.
[6] Daniel 7:13.
[7] Jeremiah 30:7.
[8] Daniel 9:26.
[9] Daniel 10:14.

gain world popularity whose "deadly wound was healed."[10] All the world will wonder after this beast, as he is called. His evil character and reign are described in the 13th chapter of the Book of Revelation in the New Testament. He will inspire people to worship the Dragon or Satan and he will be given a mouth to speak great things and will delight in blaspheming God. This beast will make war with the people of God and he will be given power over all the nations. All the world will worship him, whose names are not written in the Book of Life. He will cause everyone to receive a mark in their right hand or in their forehead. No man will be able to buy or sell without this mark, or the name of the beast, or the number of his name. That number, the Scripture tells us, is the number of a man which is six hundred, threescore and six, or 666."[11]

One observant boy stood to his feet and said, "But sir, 666 adds up to 18 or Hai, the number of life. To us Jews, it would appear to be a good thing."

"Hmm, a very interesting point," Jay said before continuing. "The spirit of deception will be at work to fool multitudes, for the Scripture says:

> And he doeth great wonders, so that
> he maketh fire come down from heaven
> on earth in the sight of men and DECEIVETH
> them that dwell on the earth.[12]

"Perhaps many may think him to be Elijah. Anyone taking his number will be eternally lost, the Scriptures tell us. He will initiate a world system of buying and selling whereby every person will be forced to have this number."

"What makes you think this is going to happen in our lifetime?" Gidi, the Israeli who introduced Jay to the group, asked. He felt protective toward the students.

---

[10] Relevation 13: 3, 12.
[11] Revelation 13: 18.
[12] Revelation 13: 13, 14.

"Today is God's time to favor and build up Zion, Zion being His city, Jerusalem; His land, Israel; His people, the Jews. The psalmist wrote:

> Thou shalt arise and have mercy on Zion,
> For the time to favour her, yea, the set
> time is come.
>
> For Thy servants take pleasure in her stones,
>
> And favour the dust thereof.
> When the Lord shall build up Zion,
> He shall appear in His glory,
>
> This shall be written for the generation to come.[13]

"In Hebrew, 'the generation to come' reads 'dor acharon,' 'the last generation.' I'm sure you will agree that Zion is being built up today! Only in Israel do people lovingly care for stones and sift the dust of numerous ancient sites, in the hopes of finding some link with the past.

"If you visit Jerusalem today, you will see that tremendous excavations have taken place around the walls of the Old City wherever it has been possible. Presently, great interest is being generated by the digs in the City of David, south of the Temple Mount. I think you will all agree with me that the Lord has built up Zion. He gave her a second birth in 1948 so that once again He could 'appear in His glory' to bless not just Israel, but the entire world.

"Jesus said:

> 'So also ye, when ye see these things
> come to pass, know ye that the kingdom
> of God is near. Truly, I say unto you
> that this generation shall not pass
> away till all these things be fulfilled.'"[14]

---

[13] Psalm 102: 13, 14, 16, 18.
[14] Luke 21: 31, 32.

Gidi stood to his feet. "It is true that in our generation we have seen Israel restored and much more. Jay, we thank you for coming and speaking so frankly with us; I'm sure, though, there are many questions."

The students did have many questions, and the majority of them were unaware of the "signs of the times" written by their prophets. Perhaps the most important thing Jay accomplished was to challenge these young men with keen bright minds, to go back to the original source, their very own Scriptures,.and read all the prophets carefully!

Much later Gidi again stood to his feet and said, "It is now 10 p.m. and our families will be looking for us. Let's conclude our meeting with 'Am Israel Hai.' "[15]

Everyone was on their feet, singing with loud enthusiasm. As Jay bid his farewell, he could see Israel coming to life right before his eyes. Their songs of victory followed him out into the street!

AUSTRALIA

[15] 'The people of Israel live.'

Jay Rawlings
AFRICA

14
The Garden Sanctuary

A household servant, also a believer, asked Jay to visit Oscar, who was suffering from leukemia.

Jay drove up the sweeping circular drive to the mansion not knowing what to expect. Another kindly servant came and answered the door. "He is waiting for you," she said and invited Jay into the foyer. Toys were strewn all over the floor. Three little children were playing hide-and-seek amongst the white and turquoise furniture of a formal sitting room. She led Jay through this room into the family room at a lower level. Everything spelled comfort — the soft sofas, rich carpets, grand piano, stone fireplace and background music.

Oscar, dressed in tweeds and patent leather loafers, came forward with his hand extended. Jay introduced himself. The ill man's hair was streaked with gray, his sideburns were snow-white, and although his smile was warm and his skin tanned, he did not look well. As they grasped hands, Jay commented, "There's a gentle presence in your home."

"Yes," Oscar replied, "God has been good to me. Come with me and let me show you where I talk to Him."

He opened sliding doors and the men walked out onto a tranquil scene of rolling lawns and gardens, set around a swimming pool. The wind played in the leaves of trees which had been thoughtfully planted. "This is my synagogue," he said. They strolled under the trees and Oscar talked as though he had known Jay all of his life. "I don't know how I became successful," he continued. "I never tried; it just came to me. I always wanted to do the right thing. My kids tell me I'm a millionaire, but I started out by going to university riding my bike. I used to work at lunchtime in an office at noon, just to make lunch money." Oscar readily related several experiences that had brought success with the years.

Then he stood still and began in a serious tone, "For thirty years I've played soccer at lunchtime with my cronies to keep in shape. All of a sudden, I couldn't run very well. The doctors took blood tests, and told me that I had a blood disease. I said, 'I don't want to know anything about it. I don't feel bad; just cure me and make me well again. Just tell me I'm well.'" There was a pleading in his voice. "That, as you know, was some time ago." Desperation filled Oscar's eyes; he quickly lowered them.

"I've come to pray," Jay said.

"Please go ahead."

"Oscar," Jay said, "we're going to ask for a miracle of divine healing. God spoke to the children of Israel just after they crossed the Red Sea and said,

> If thou wilt diligently hearken to the voice
> of the Lord thy God, and wilt do that which
> is right in His sight, and wilt give ear to
> His commandments, and keep all His statutes,
> I will put none of these diseases upon thee,
> which I have brought upon the Egyptians:
> for I am the Lord that healeth thee.[1]

Oscar, I understand that you are terminally ill."

"Yes, yes, I am — it's no secret," he agreed, meeting Jay's gaze.

"The Scriptures are filled with consolation. May I read a couple of verses from Psalms?"

---

[1] Exodus 15: 26.

"Please, go ahead."
"Maybe you'd like to repeat them after me, Oscar."

In the day of my trouble I sought the Lord:
my sore ran in the night, and ceased not:
my soul refused to be comforted.
I remembered God.[2]

For I will declare mine iniquity;
I will be sorry for my sin.

Make haste to help me,
O Lord my salvation.[3]

Oscar made the Scriptures his own personal petition as he slowly repeated them.

Jay continued, "I have based every decision I make on the fact that there is power and authority in the Name of the Lord. Our part is to be honest and call for help. When we ask for bread, He doesn't give us a stone."

Oscar searched Jay's face. Desperation rose to the surface of his emotions; he began to cry. "I don't know why I'm crying like this, I'm sobbing like a baby. I'm so scared, I don't know what to do, I feel all tight."

"Let's pray, Oscar," Jay said, putting his arm around the trembling man.

Gradually the tightness left Oscar's chest and he relaxed. In no time he began to pray on his own. "May it be Your will to heal me completely, yet if it is determined that I die, I will accept it at Your hand with love. Father of the fatherless and Judge of the widow, protect my beloved ones." Tears continued to course down Oscar's cheeks as he prayed. The "Peace" of God that passes all understanding flooded Oscar's weakened body and soul as the tension and fear evaporated. Peace filled the garden synagogue as well.

[2] Psalm 77: 2, 3.
[3] Psalm 38: 18, 22.

The men continued to sit quietly by the pool enjoying the anointing that had come down. Time held no meaning.

"You know," Oscar volunteered, "in 1960 I visited Israel and had dinner with Ben Gurion. That night he put his hand on my shoulder and looked me square in the eye and said, 'You should come here and be an architect.' What do you think of that?" he asked.

"Well, I agree with Mr. Ben Gurion," Jay said. "Why not do your building in Israel?"

Oscar lapsed into silence for a long time. "What can I do for you?" he said as he studied Jay closely. His face was filled with gratitude. "Could you use my country house, or a car? Please, what is it I can do for you?"

"Go to the Land, Oscar," Jay hugged him. "Go and build a new life in the Land."

AFRICA

15
Memories

Documented facts and photographs in the Holocaust Museum in Jerusalem sickened Doug Phillips as he toured the memorial to the six million Jews slaughtered during World War II. Doug asked himself, "How could any human being treat another like this?" He had been profoundly moved by his visit which was to affect his future. When university examinations were ended in May, he visited Europe on his way back to California. Doug had decided to see "for himself."

Modern Poland has a virtual absence of Jews, with just ten thousand as opposed to three and a half million before World War II. The Polish people attach great importance to their history under Nazi occupation, evidenced in the memorials all over Warsaw, in Auschwitz, Treblinka and in the maps showing the hundreds of places in Poland where the Nazis carried out mass executions, indicating the numbers killed in each place. Glancing at his map, Doug realized that Poland is a Christian as well as a Jewish graveyard.

Ten o'clock in the morning Doug's train pulled into the Warsaw station. He had been travelling all night, but was so desirous of visiting the Jewish community that he felt no tiredness. The summer sun warmed him as he looked for the community. It was not hard to find. The Rabbi invited him in for tea and explained that the other synagogues had been converted into movie theaters. It seemed to Doug that the memories of the past continued to take their toll on the Rabbi's mind and body. He wore heaviness as if it were an overcoat.

"Sir," Doug began over tea, "why don't you come home to Israel?"

"I'm well able," he replied, "but I need to stay here. My people need a Rabbi."

After tea he took Doug to visit various men of his community. It was obvious that this Rabbi was a shepherd to the broken ones, the castoff, unwanted men. Together they visited men living with various afflictions that had resulted from years spent in concentration camps during World War II. Limbs had been amputated at the knee; the mutilated men hobbled about on wooden blocks. Unlike their Western counterparts, Polish survivors of the Holocaust receive no reparations. Other men were crippled, scarred, deaf or blind. The one thing they all had in common was the numbers tattooed into their left forearms. The poor men were shabbily dressed; now, past retirement age, their pensions were very meager. Like their Rabbi, they too were shrouded in black memories that literally sapped the life from them. Memories of pain and horror, hatred and death. . . . Doug felt sick to his stomach. He wanted to sob.

At noon an English-speaking Jew from the synagogue, named Eli Fogel, invited Doug to the community house for lunch. The invitation was meaningful to Doug because of a dream he had had the month before, in which he was invited by a Jew to lunch. Eli was the man in his dream.

Once seated at the lunch table, Doug began, "Eli, I'm sorry to see the men here still suffering intensely from their ordeal of years ago."

"You are right, the torturous memories are killing them," Eli agreed, only to be interrupted by Doug who insisted upon finishing all that he had to say. Eli closed his mouth and listened to the fiery young stranger who had sized up the situation within minutes.

"Do you realize," Doug's eyes were ablaze, "that Jeremiah in speaking of the return to Zion said,

> '... and with them the blind and the lame, the woman with child and her that travaileth with child together: a great company shall return thither. They shall come with weeping, and with supplications will I lead them....' "[1]

He paused, drew a breath and continued, "They come weeping out of the nations where they have been hideously abused. Their memories are too painful for any man to erase, but God says He will lead them out. Don't you see?" Doug pleaded. "These people have got to come out; they have no life here." He paused and took a sip of water.

"Daniel saw visions of what would come against his people in the last days, and he fainted and was sick afterward. He speaks of a prince that shall come, but not the Messiah; he speaks of how many will be deceived and lost. You must stir the people. Israel is your home. I cannot imagine why you would hesitate to go, knowing the Word."

It was not his words that shook Eli as much as the fact that the words came from a 19-year-old youth.

Doug's lunch sat before him cold and untouched. Everyone else at the table had finished. He had no appetite. His hands and feet were cold, he was shivering and felt sick. "Oh, that I might stir these Jews to move," was all Doug could think.

It was time to leave for the train station. The two men walked back to the train. Before boarding Doug turned to face Eli and put his hands on the Polish Jew's shoulders.

"What *are* you doing here?" Doug looked into his eyes.

Eli stared back, blinked, and swallowed hard. "Nothing," was his quiet reply.

"Then be quick, come to Israel," Doug pleaded.

---

[1] Jeremiah 31:8, 9.

The whistle blew, it was time to get aboard. Doug climbed the steps of the coach, threw himself into a seat and waved goodbye to Eli. "If only they would listen," he was crying now. His heart ached, and so did his stomach. The haunting faces of the men he had met earlier that day filled his mind. It was not their mutilated bodies which troubled Doug as much as the obvious pain that had stamped itself indelibly upon their countenances. Memories, Doug thought to himself, so ugly and demonic, possessed and tormented them, destroying any joy and hope that might try to arise in their hearts . . . silent hunters of the past still stalking innocent prey.

POLAND

16
Sammy the Sabra

The Côte d'Azur is the playground of Europe. Blue Mediterranean waters lap against sand beaches and cliffs ranging in color from chalk white to rose red. Tall cedars and pines hide precariously perched white villas which command magnificent vistas out over the sea. Yachts from all over the world bob at anchor in the gentle coves and inlets. Having just arrived from extensive travels in South America, Jay had settled the boys and I into an 11th-century stone village located in the hills just behind Nice. We enjoyed the company of the country folk in the village. We also established contact with Jews who, along with thousands of other tourists, had come to the Riviera to sun and swim. We found Jews in Menton, Monaco, Nice, Cannes, Antibes, Jean le Pin and St. Tropez.

At the seaside in Cannes, women sat bare-breasted, sunning and playing cards. Their bronzed skin and hard facial expressions suggested a life of boredom and seemed to say, "You couldn't possibly have anything new to tell us. . . ." We found some of the best places to meet Jews were in the small cafés situated right down on the beaches, only a few meters from the surf.

Sammy, a Jerusalemite, the son of a scribe, was one of thousands who had come to get away from it all. Clerking in the big-name hotels in Cannes brought in good money and lots of opportunity for an eligible bachelor to be fussy about his choice of a date.

Sammy was shrewd, clever, good with languages, full of mischief, but most unsettling of all, he still found himself a little religious. On one such religious occasion, he just happened to be at the Cannes Jewish community center of the Côte d'Azur. He moved easily among the tanned and beautiful.

French, Spanish, Italian, German and English were spoken as he floated from one cluster of conversation to another in the community center. ". . .Every Jew belongs in Israel. . . ." That phrase caught his attention, so he drifted in the direction of the conversation.

"Hmm," he thought to himself, "a Zionist, but doesn't know what he's talking about!"

"Yes," the bearded North American continued, "We're travelling to the various communities of Europe, telling the leaders to encourage their people to return to Israel."

Sammy studied the face of the man doing the talking. His thoughts ran on, "Looks sincere, but what's in it for him?"

Pushing himself forward, he said, "Hi, I'm Sammy."

The response was warm and immediate, "I'm glad to meet you; I'm Jay." Their conversation continued for several minutes and then the formal function of the evening began.

"Why don't you come to visit us sometime?" Jay offered. "We live in a delightful village just up in the mountains behind Nice. Perhaps you could help us with Hebrew?"

"Why not? I'd be glad to," responded Sammy.

"Great, next Wednesday, at seven?" asked Jay.

"Sure," was Sammy's flip reply.

Wednesday at dusk a week later found Sammy driving up the Var Valley to the old stone village of Carros. Walking from the parking lot up well-worn stone steps to the house, Sammy decided that he would be cool and self-sufficient.

The light and warmth of the French Provincial kitchen

welcomed him in and made him instantly forget his hasty resolution.

"Come in, Sammy, and I'll introduce you to our friends." Jay held the door open. "First of all, this is Doug Phillips. Doug has been visiting Poland and Yugoslavia this summer. He studied Hebrew in Jerusalem last year and is pretty good."

"Shalom." Doug rose from the small handmade stool he was sitting on and grinned at Sammy.

"The beautiful blonde is Julia Tooley from New Zealand. We met her in Vienna — guess where — the Great Synagogue of course. Julia has also lived in Israel and is here for just a couple of days. George," called Jay, "come and meet Sammy." Jay walked over to the corner of the room and pulled a very shy man with pink cheeks and large mustache to his feet. "George is a native here and lives downstairs."

"Bon soir, monsieur," George said sweetly, and blushed a bright pink.

"These two girls," Jay said pointing to them, "have been all over Europe encouraging the likes of you to go home, Sheila and Jill."

"Welcome," said Sheila, pulling out a chair from around the heavy wooden table," come and join us."

"David, Chris and Joshua are my three boys. Come and say 'Shalom,' guys," called Jay. At that the boys left their toys and shyly came and stood around their Dad. "And Sammy, the best thing I ever did was marry Meridel, and here she is!"

"It's nice meeting you," I squeezed his hand, then gathered up the little boys for bed.

"Sammy, it's all yours," encouraged Jay, completing the circle around the table.

For a minute he was quiet, self-conscious. "I didn't know that people like you existed," Sammy confessed. "Do you all live here?"

"No," Doug spoke up. "We just drop in on our way to other places. There happens to be a tribe of us just now." As

Sammy's first Hebrew lesson progressed, he realized that he hadn't seen people with such an interest in their studies since his days in Yeshiva. His assessment was that these people were keen Hebrew students. After the work session, the evening came to a happy conclusion with everyone singing the songs of Zion. "They really enjoy this," Sammy thought as he sat listening with his eyes closed. He was reminded of his ailing father in Jerusalem when Doug suggested they end with,

> He hath shewed thee, O man, what is good;
> And what doth the Lord require of thee,
> But to do justly, and to love mercy,
> And to walk humbly with thy God.[1]

"What is it about them," Sammy wondered. "What is it I see on their faces and feel as they speak and sing?" he mused to himself. "How did they know that my father quoted this to me every day of my life?" Sammy could feel himself getting upset, a little emotional, longing for something in life that just never materialized.

About ten o'clock he left the group with many good wishes showered upon him. Jay strolled down to the plaza with him. The full moon and stars shone as pure as silver against the black night.

"Come on, let's climb up to the moulin for a better view of the valley," Jay suggested. Sammy raced him to the hill. When they reached the top breathless, Jay pointed to the surrounding landscape shimmering in the moonlight.

"Those peaks are the Italian Alps, the Var Valley winds down there at your feet and the Mediterranean is to your right."

"It certainly is a beautiful night," Sammy volunteered, making small talk.

---

[1] Micah 6:8.

"Sammy," Jay began, "I don't mean to pry, but I believe you have a great heritage in Jerusalem. Why don't you go home and do something with it? How many Hebrew scribes are there in the world today?"

Sammy's silence was his answer. What could he honestly say. As he looked up into the night, he became oblivious to everything. A vision formed before his eyes as the stars faded from sight. The black sky became the backdrop for the following drama: Sammy's father stood bowing and weeping, kissing the stones of the Western Wall in Jerusalem . . . . The chanting prayer coming from his father's lips seemed to lay itself about Sammy's shoulders as a prayer shawl possessing him. He could not shake it off. Offered in simplicity and humility, his father's prayer asked God that his son would come and stand with him as a scribe in Jerusalem.

Jay's question remained unanswered for many minutes, and then came Sammy's faint reply. "I know, I should go," he confessed, "I will . . . ."

FRANCE

Jay Rawlings
Meridel Rawlings
CANADA

17
A Jerusalemite in Quebec

Canada's province of Quebec boasts a Jewish community of 120,000, about half the total of all Jews in the nation. It was fall and Jay and I had begun a tour to various Jewish communities across Canada. In Montreal we attended synagogue and were publicly welcomed by Rabbi Langner who introduced the three of us as "Joshua Rawlings and his parents from Israel." Joshua, a busy three-year-old at the time, was delighted, and waved to the Rabbi from the congregation. David and Chris were in Hebrew school in Haifa, Israel. A very warm and interested congregation greeted us at the Kiddush following the service. There was much talk of growing opposition to Quebec separatism which used Bill 101, the provincial language law making French the only official language in the Province of Quebec, as the catalyst for eliminating all signs of English. Several thousand Jews had already sold their homes and businesses to move to English-speaking cities across Canada.

Later in the week we travelled north on "Voyageur" coach lines to Quebec City, Canada's only walled city. The historic gates reminded us of the Old City of Jerusalem. An old friend, Bob Foster, had invited us to come. It had been three years since Bob had carrolled with us on Christmas Eve in our quaint 11th-century village on the Riviera. The reserved patois speaking people loved our music. He was a French major at the university in Nice at the time; and was now doing graduate work at LaValle University.

Joshua was sound asleep by the time we pulled into the bus depot. Bob met us with warm hugs and instantly it was like old times again. He helped us carry the luggage through a brightly lit shopping mall and explained, "I've made arrangements for you to stay with a very loving French Canadian family. David is a butcher and he and his wife are known for their hospitality. First, I want you to meet some of our friends from the church." We stopped directly in front of a pet shop... the buff-colored spaniel puppies in the window were huddled into one corner of the large cage, sound asleep. Bob led us up a stairway filled with nasty odors from the pet shop. Friends met us at the top of the stairs and took us into a large room filled with French Canadians engaged in their weekly Bible study. The first thing that caught our eye was the Israeli flag hanging on one of the walls. Students, laborers, simple housewives and retired people were seated in a circle with Bibles open on their knees. Bob introduced us as Canadians living in Israel. A young girl with long, flaming red hair greeted us in Hebrew and announced, "in honor of our friends, we are going to sing a Hebrew song." The minute Louise struck the first chord on her guitar it was very evident that she was an artist. Everyone joined in:

Oseh shalom bi-m'romav,
Hu ya-aseh shalom aleinu,
V'al kol Yisrael,
V'imru, imru amen.

He who makes peace in His heavens
Will make peace on us,
And on all Israel;
And say Amen.

"Jay," Bob asked, "I know it's late, but please tell us something about Israel. We pray daily for the Peace of Jerusalem."

He handed the meeting over to Jay who shared our personal experiences living in a Jewish neighborhood and studying Hebrew with all that that entails. After the group was dismissed, Louise, the young girl who greeted us in Hebrew and song, came and offered her time and assistance during our stay in the city. "We all," she explained, "belong to a church congregation of 1000 French Canadians who are keen to learn more about Israel." We learned later that Louise had been a nightclub singer in Montreal from the age of ten to sixteen years until Jesus walked into her life in a very personal way. Now a Bible student, she was composing Hebraic music in her spare moments and shared with her colleagues all that she could glean from Scripture and reference books on Judaism. She had sung on the "700 Club" and "100 Huntley Street" Christian T.V. networks in the U.S.A. and Canada.

Bob led us back out into the biting cold October wind which was driving large flakes of snow onto the frozen ground. The wind stung our faces and legs. The temperature had dropped below freezing and we shivered trying not to let our teeth chatter. We were warmed by thoughts of the precious and sincere people we had met this night. Bob had led us to a hearthside whose warmth penetrated right to one's soul. Arrangements were made the following day to meet the young visionary pastor of this church body. Allen Bowen opened his Congregation and Bible School to us to share the importance of why Christians must support their local Jews and Israel.

Later in the week, Louise helped us get in touch with the local Rabbi. She had never met him personally but had encouraged the congregation to pray for him and for his people. We introduced ourselves to him by telephone. Consequently he cordially invited us to come and visit him. By the time the bus dropped us off at the door of the synagogue, we were chilled to the bone. The Rabbi was waiting for us with the door open and called out, "Shalom." He seated us near the warm air vents in the vestibule of the synagogue.

Jay began, "We live in Israel and are just not dressed for a real Canadian winter...." The Rabbi chuckled.

"Here," he offered, "take your coats off and put them by the heat so you'll be warm when it's time to go outside again." He was a small, sensitive man with dark, delicate features and very white skin. His hands were those of a scholar. "May I ask why you have come?" he inquired.

"Yes," Jay cleared his throat and smiled, "we are Christians living in Israel now and are on a journey across Canada to encourage the various communities to consider afresh the challenge of moving to Israel to live."

I don't think the Rabbi heard one word after the word "CHRISTIAN." It seemed to choke him. He became visibly upset and eyed us with contempt. He struggled with his emotions and in spite of himself began to rant and rave.... "The New Testament is the biggest hoax in the world today; Jesus the greatest imposter, and he is surely No God! Such a view is pagan and blasphemous. Why, the New Testament is full of error. Take the Palm Sunday procession, when all the people waved palm branches... anyone with any sense knows that we only use palm branches for the Feast of Tabernacles. Obviously they got their festivals all mixed up." Jay and I sat motionless. It helped to remember that this Rabbi lived in a closed traditional Catholic community, and he may never have had a kind word spoken to him from people he knew as "Christian."

Barely taking time to draw a breath, he continued, "Take a look at history. Christians have slaughtered Jews in the name of God." Jay and I exchanged glances and held our peace. "Read the history books," the Rabbi continued. "Nonsense. What you Christians believe is absolute nonsense." He then quietened down and seemed somewhat satisfied, having gotten it off his chest.

As a mother would address a little boy, I began slowly and distinctly, "First of all, I'm sure there is reason for your bitterness, but I'm afraid you are addressing it unjustly. You see, there is all the difference in the world between people who come from a so-called Christian nation, or who even call themselves Christian, and people who are 'born-again' Christians. You will know real Christians by their attitude toward Israel. It's really very simple. For it is impossible to say that you love God and then turn around and hate His people. Rabbi, I'm so glad we've come today. We want to introduce you to a group of French Christians who are *real* Zionists!"

With that I gave him a big smile and continued, "I've known Jesus since I was just a little girl and I love Him. Even greater than that, He loves me, and He answers me when I speak to Him. He came to love us and show us an example of how it is possible to live without condemnation. Because I know just how much He has helped me, I'm not ashamed of Him."

The Rabbi was listening attentively and I felt liberty in speaking. "In His Name I've seen blind eyes opened and deaf ears unstopped! I've prayed and seen women whose breasts were filled with cancer healed. You may not understand it. I don't understand it, but it works. There is medical proof to back what I'm saying to you. The Spirit of the Living God told us to come and see you today. We speak of the Ruach Ha-Kodesh as the comforter who brings peace in the midst of confusion and trouble."

The Rabbi swallowed, his black eyes lost their fire and were sad. "Say," he said quietly, coming a step closer to us, "I've got a rotten temper. Would you pray for me?"

"Yes," Jay broke in. "May we pray in Jesus' Name?"

"No, no, I couldn't do that." The Rabbi hesitated, his words were filled with sadness.

"Well, we *will* be praying for you," Jay assured him. "You know," I said, a new thought coming into my mind, "you are going to wake up one night and the Lord is going to tell you to go home to Israel." Jay reached out and touched the Rabbi's arm, and smiled kindly into his troubled face.

"Oh, oh, well," the Rabbi began to fidget, pulling his arm

from beneath Jay's hand. "He hasn't spoken to me yet!" He sounded as if he were relieved. Then he continued proudly, "Did you know that I was born in Jerusalem?"

"How wonderful," I said. "You are one of those precious people written about in the Psalms. 'The Lord shall count, when he writeth up the people, that this man was born there.' "[1]

"How long ago did you leave?" Jay asked quietly.

"Oh, ever since I was a child," the Rabbi shared.

"Well, I want to encourage you to keep listening," Jay said. "One day the Lord may call you to come home!" We felt very close to one another now in spite of a deep sadness that had filled the vestibule of that synagogue.

We left quietly.

That was many years ago and since our initial visit with the Rabbi, he has welcomed Louise and many other young French Christians into his own home for evenings of Hebrew conversations and Hebrew music. He encouraged several of the Quebecers to come to Israel. It was our privilege to welcome Louise, along with Bruno and Lynne, a young couple from the same church, to Jerusalem. Louise excelled in her Hebrew studies and wrote many beautiful songs while inspired on our rooftop in the Old City of Jerusalem. She created musicals for Purim and the Feast of Tabernacles. The church young people sang and played out biblical themes *highly* enjoyed by *our* Rabbi in Quebec City who invited them to perform in his synagogue. Today Louise is becoming a popular performer in Montreal and New York.

CANADA

---

[1] Psalm 87:6.

Yossi Hochman
ISRAEL

18
Victims of Terror

"I am a rebel and freedom is my cause."

Yasir Arafat
U.N. General Assembly
October 1974

It was Saturday, March 11, 1978.

This Shabbat had been no different from other quiet Shabbats spent in our home situated on Mount Carmel in Haifa. We enjoyed living in sight of a 270-degree panorama of the Haifa harbor. From the sunroom one could gaze out over the Lebanese hills all the way to Mount Hermon. Occasionally the boom of a gun could be heard from 30 miles distance on the Lebanese border. In the garden pigeons nestled in tall Alexandria palms. Their incessant cooing blended with the rustling of warm Mediterranean breezes through bright green palm fronds. Today was quiet, except for the occasional laughter of children that penetrated up to our window from beautiful Yefe Nof Street, the panorama drive of Haifa.

David, our ten-year-old, was the first to tell us the terrible news. He came bounding up the stairs shouting, "Mom!" Breathlessly he burst forth, "A bus has been hit by terrorists—Roni said so, it's heading for Tel Aviv... quick, turn on the radio." Having delivered the message, he collapsed on a kitchen stool. Immediately I switched on the radio and began searching for news. It was 4 p.m. The newscaster began:

"Earlier this afternoon a band of terrorists entered the beach area near Kibbutz Ma'agan Michael and seized a bus; a roadblock has been set up near the Country Club, north of Tel Aviv. The terrorists arrived in two rubber boats and are heavily armed. We believe there were two acts of terrorism. A bus full of people on a Shabbat outing was attacked. Until now we have no more details. The police announced that the coastal road and Geha road are closed to the public."

By nightfall news of the tragedy had blanketed Israel with sadness. All that remained of the bus was a charred ruin of tangled metal splattered with the blood of adults and children. Many were dead.

David and Chris returned to school at David Yellin Elementary the following day. Our boys were sobered by the announcement that a memorial service would be held in memory of six children from their school who had died in the bus incident.

It was 15 months later when we were filming "Apples of Gold" that I arranged the interview with Yossi Hochman at his home on Kibbutz Neve Yam. Yossi had lost his wife and two sons and his legs in that terrible bus incident.

His bungalow had been renovated to accommodate a wheelchair. Fiercely independent, Yossi insisted on serving us cool refreshments himself. Touching photos of himself and his lovely wife, Rifka, hung on the walls. A family photo album lay open on the coffee table. We felt like intruders while looking at the photos of loving family scenes. His personal loss somehow became ours. Yossi, blond and muscular in the prime of life, wheeled himself into the living room to join us. The stumps of both legs were bandaged as he was fighting a slight infection.

Jay was the interviewer in the film and gave Yossi instructions in Hebrew. "Yossi, forget the cameras. Try not to let the lights bother you. I'll ask pertinent questions, okay?" Yossi nodded. Bruce Allen, director, called "Silence on set"—the camera whirred as Yossi told his own story.

"On the way back home about six miles from our kibbutz we were attacked by terrorists. The bus was hit and so we stopped. A few people were killed but we didn't know what was happening. After a few minutes the terrorists pulled up in a taxi. They shouted, 'Get back on the bus.' The terrorists ordered us to turn the bus around and head in the direction of Tel Aviv. We were ordered to close the curtains of the bus and not to speak or shout. The entire time the terrorists screamed 'Palestine, Palestine.' I thought they were under the influence of drugs, but I was mistaken, they were not drugged, they were brainwashed. They were just kids 16 or 17 years old and very easily rattled.

"Rifka, my wife, Ro'i, 6½ years, and Ilan, 3 years, behaved ideally. I sat on the floor of the bus; my hands behind my back were untied. I will never forget it. I remember every detail. We arrived at the crossroads next to the Country Club. The bus stopped and we were caught in crossfire between terrorists and Israeli security forces. The bus was bombed and turned into a massive bloodbath. A friend of mine, sitting two seats in front of me, quickly snatched a gun from one of the terrorists. He hit two terrorists standing at the entrance to the bus. Suddenly I came to the conclusion that it was time to do something; so I jumped on one of the terrorists, snatched his Russian weapon (Klatchnikov) out of his hands, and shot him. He dropped to the floor and I saw another terrorist pointing his gun at me. I kicked him in the chest, and shot him. Somebody shouted, 'Everybody out' as the front of the bus was clear of terrorists. I turned to Rifka and the children when a hand grenade exploded. After the explosion there was silence and I saw Rifka and the boys lying on the floor of the bus, dead.

"I didn't know what to do. I couldn't stand on my legs, blood was pouring from me. Should I stay on the bus with my loved ones or get off? I believe that the power of life is the most powerful force given to man. I don't know how to explain it. I started to crawl toward the front of the bus and realized I couldn't get down, my feet had been blown off. I was helped off the bus and crawled 10 meters in the direction of the bushes.

"The bus was in flames. The terrorists fired a bazooka at it and then began a serious exchange of fire with the security forces.

"A small four-year-old girl near me was wandering around in shock. I don't know how I managed it after what I had been through, but I grabbed her and sat her next to me. Because of this motion, one of the terrorists saw where we were and threw a grenade at us. It fell three meters from me and exploded.

"I arrived at the hospital with just one pint of blood left in my body; I remained fully conscious. I knew exactly what had happened to Rifka, Ro'i and Ilan. I knew there were two options open to me, either to carry on or to go backward. I knew I had to carry on in spite of all I had lost.

"Those first months of recuperation I fought with superhuman powers. I was in a bad way, but never did I think I had nothing to live for. Both of my legs were amputated, but I said to myself, 'I *will* stand on my feet!'

"It was a Thursday that Dr. S. Sternbach brought in the artificial limbs. He fitted the limbs on me and said, 'Get up!' I looked at him and did! I stood on the two limbs and started walking. I remember it was a rare thing; the lady psychotherapist started crying. Today I walk much better, but then I walked without support too.

"I continue to work and enjoy my job as social coordinator for the staff of Egged Bus Lines in Haifa. I still remember Rifka now as I remembered her then. I'm not escaping from reality, but it's as if I can see them in front of me now. I had wonderful kids. We raised them as we were raised. Rifka was quiet, educated and broad-minded.

"Ro'i, the oldest, used to go with me everywhere, to every soccer game that I played in, excursions, hunting... everywhere. Ilan, the youngest, was healthy and outstanding among kids his own age. They received their qualities partly from me and from their wonderful mother, so intelligent and even-tempered."

When the interview ended, we were very very quiet. What could one say?

"You know," Yossi began, "people wonder why I'm not in a mental hospital. Everybody on the bus lost somebody. I wish the terrorists would fight men—not our women and children. Now, I don't wear black and I'm not religious, but I do know that God listens to hear what comes out of my mouth. I don't understand why this happened to me, I *can't* understand it, but, it's all right in my heart, it's all right!"

Jay smiled at the truth of his confession. "You know, Yossi," he said, "Abraham didn't have a synagogue to go to. It was his faith in God that brought him to this Land. His life was built around a relationship with God. Don't you suppose that he felt something when he looked out over the Land? I believe that he felt God's pleasure shower down over him. You described it as being alright in your heart. You see, Yossi, the correct response of our heart and soul is really what it's all about. When we say and do things that please Him, we can actually sense the presence of His Spirit with us."

Joshua, our five-year-old, drifted silently over to Yossi and laid his small head on his chest. Chris moved closer, instinctively wanting to comfort, and took one of his hands. David came and stood close enough to the wheelchair to allow Yossi to put his arm around him. As they conversed freely in Hebrew, Yossi soon had the boys giggling. In the warmth of his love they didn't notice his bandaged limbs or wheelchair. Yossi was beaming too. Seeing them together brought pain to my heart and tears to my eyes. He had lost so much. I rejected the question, "Why?" that tried to force its way into my mind.

Looking up from the boys to the film crew, Yossi announced, "I'm constructing a memorial garden here in the kibbutz." He proudly showed us the model—complete with paddling pool, tennis courts and fountains. "My family and I decided that we didn't want a memorial statue, but a garden. I want it to be a place of commemoration where children and their parents will enjoy family times together."

Captured PLO terrorist later explaining his orders for the blood bus mission.

Question: What was your mission?

PLO Terrorist: Our mission was to land on the Israeli coast and kill as large a number of old men, women, children and babies as possible . . . all those found on the way.

Question: Civilians?

PLO Terrorist: Yes, civilians.

Question: And to kill?

PLO Terrorist: Yes, old men, women and children, whoever we would find on the way.[1]

Fatah terrorists killed 35 people and wounded 82 in this bus attack.

ISRAEL

[1] Quoted from "The PLO" film produced by Hilla Films, Switzerland, 1979.

Jay Rawlings
Meridel Rawlings
THE PEOPLE'S REPUBLIC OF CHINA

19
The Great Wall

Beijing, or "Northern Peace," has been the capital of China for a period spanning almost seven hundred years. Today it is the political, cultural and administrative center of a resurgent China, home of eight million citizens, headquarters of the Communist Party and seat of the government.

In comparison to the other cities we visited, where the Chinese had been curious and even friendly, we found the atmosphere in Beijing strained. Here the people kept their distance, unsmiling.

That first day we were taken to one of the world-famous Peking restaurants for a sumptuous banquet of "Peking Duck," the specialty of the house. Blue smoke filled the restaurant while old-fashioned ceiling fans circled lazily overhead. All the tables were crowded with Chinese families enjoying Sunday lunch. Their unfriendly stares made us feel like intruders. Jay, wearing his auto-harp, stepped in through the door ahead of us, and struck a melodious chord. The steady buzz of conversation stopped, and immediately the place was quiet. We weren't quite sure if it was the instrument or Jay's red beard that demanded their attention. Together we all sang in Mandarin, "China is a good land." Little children hid their faces in the sleeves of parental Mao-jackets, but the grownups obviously loved the music and applauded after the first tune, until we sang a second one. We continued to sing as we walked upstairs to our dining room. The atmosphere had completely changed and the Chinese grinned openly at us.

China is a paradise for antique collectors. The guides took this into account and arranged a visit to the Antique Shops right after lunch. We welcomed the opportunity to get out into the streets among the people.

Jay continued to carry his harp and sing to the children as he walked past. I went on ahead into an art supply shop. A Western couple in the back of the shop exclaimed, "My God, what's that?" as Jay entered, accompanied by the short rotund member of the tour who insisted upon wearing his large homemade wooden cross. "Oh brother," I thought to myself, and kept my back turned.

Jay went straight over to the couple and said, "Hi, I'm Jay Rawlings from Jerusalem. You're Jewish, aren't you?"

The couple was stunned! "Ah, yes, hello,' the man spoke first, reservedly. "I'm Ed from Montreal and my wife, Pamela, who is from Toronto. Yes, we're Jewish."

"What are you doing in Peking?" Jay asked, his friendliness putting them at ease.

"We're teaching English at two different universities," Ed volunteered.

"Great!" Jay was obviously enthused. "Darling," he beckoned to me, "come and meet our new friends."

I obediently ventured near. "Shalom," I said, shaking hands. "Have you found any synagogues here?" I asked.

"Yes," Ed spoke right up, "we've found an old unused synagogue with a Star of David on it."

Pam added informatively, "During free time we visited Kaifeng, the capital of Honan Province, three hundred kilometers from here. All that remains of the community is a small road called the 'Street of the Jewish Community.' However, there are written records dating back to the 12th century with details of Jewish communities. The Jews of Kaifeng were called 'dao jin jiao' which means 'knife, nerve and religion.' Marco Polo spoke of the Jews as having political and commercial influence, and Chinese chronicles mention Jews for the first time in 1329." Pam was delighted with her discoveries and we shared her enthusiasm. It was much more rewarding to us than antique shopping; besides, our personal resources were pretty low at this point of the journey.

Sensing our interest, Pam continued, "Apparently Chinese Jews observed the Sabbath and the major Jewish Holy Days. They had Hebrew names and ate no pork."

The flow of conversation took a different direction when Jay changed the subject by asking "Have you ever been to Israel?"

Ed looked insulted. "What on earth would I go there for?" Then he added, "You know, my seventy-year-old grandfather just made aliyah to Petah Tikva. Can you believe it?"

"That was one of the first settlements in Israel," I spoke up. "In Hebrew it means 'Door of Hope.' Maybe you'll go and visit him sometime?" I suggested.

Jay leaned closer and said quietly, "We have some *Jerusalem Post* newspapers in the bottom of our suitcases..." he looked directly at Ed, "would you be interested?" He shrugged in response, "Sure, why not?"

"We also have a film on Israel with us," I ventured. Jay explained, "The Religious Research Council in Nanjing screened it just a week ago...."

"Could we see it?" Pam was interested.

"Maybe we can get it into the Beijing University?" Ed appeared genuinely enthused. We all thought it was a good idea. As we chatted, we discovered that we were all situated at the "Friendship Hotel." Ed and Pam had a room in the Residence for Foreigners Working in Beijing, and we were in the tourist section.

Later that evening, Ed found his way to our room and picked up our copy of "The Last Generation." "I'll have to get the faculty to view it first," he said. "I can't promise anything, but it's worth a try. My students would be very interested I know."

"That's really great news, Ed," Jay said, handing him a piece of paper. "Here is our telephone number. We are here till Wednesday, so keep in touch and let us know how it goes."

The days of touring flew past; our imagination was captured by the "Forbidden City." The Temple of Heaven was equally impressive. In ancient times the emperor would come here to spend a night fasting for a good harvest. The famous "Tien An Men Square," center of Beijing, occupies an area of almost one hundred acres.

Thousands upon thousands of Beijingers cycled past on wide avenues. Their dress code was uniform; men and women wore the well-known dark blue Mao-suit.

We waited with thousands of Chinese, standing six abreast, in enormously long lines, for their turn to enter the Chairman Mao Tse-tung Memorial Hall.

Filing past the body of Chairman Mao draped in the red flag of Communist China was a sobering experience. Jay pointed out that the principle which he employed, 'China first, yourself last,' is basically a spiritual principle. "But," he added, "how many millions have died under this regime of Mao's? In contrast, Jesus said, 'But seek ye first the Kingdom of God, and His righteousness; and all these things shall be added unto you.'"[1] As I stood in line I praised God inwardly that He works mightily in us, taking out self-centeredness. We have learned that He is demanding our best so that He can give us His very best, enabling us to live fruitful, meaningful lives with peace of mind. Mao's crystal coffin rests on a bier and is surrounded by flowers from all of China's provinces. His body lies in state, well preserved. Pine trees growing in ceramic pots stand like sentinels on either side of the room — Chinese symbols of longevity. I wondered how the Chinese people felt after leaving this scene. It left me feeling cold and clammy and empty. I pushed the dark thoughts from my

---

[1] Matthew 6:33.

mind and joined our group outside in the sunshine. God's sunshine!

Our trip seemed to build to a climax. We were expecting something great to happen on September 24 and it did! The famous "Ba Da Ling Pass" of the Great Wall was our destination. Excitement grew steadily from the time we boarded the train in Beijing, and continued to mount as the train entered mountainous terrain. Whe we disembarked, the air was crystal clear and cool, and the walk to the Wall was invigorating. We had personally waited for this moment for years, and at last it had come. The peak of excitement was, of course, when we stood on the Wall. It was greater than all our expectations.

Time seemed to stand still. We gazed out over the breathtaking view spread before us. Giant mountain valleys, green with lush forests, folded into one another all the way to the western horizon, as far as the eye could see. One forgot the densely crowded streets of Shanghai and Wuhan and Tienjin. There were so few people here—quietness pervaded the atmosphere. A lone hawk soared overhead.

Parts of the Wall date back to the 5th century B.C., our guide explained. More than 300,000 workmen labored for ten years to complete the work under a unified kingdom in 221 B.C. A highway was built on top of the Wall wide enough to allow a brace of five horses to gallop between the battlements. It was used to convey soldiers, arms and food with great speed to various parts of the northern kingdom. One of the wonders of the world, this three-thousand-mile, man-made phenomenon can even be seen from outer space.

It was not difficult to imagine the sound of swords clashing, arrows whistling through the air, and men crying out in agony or victory. All down through the ages wars have been fought over the Great Wall.

Following the officially guided tour, we climbed to the highest point on the Wall to make a short broadcast for

Canada's National Christian television program, "100 Huntley Street."

"Quiet on the set!" We waited for the signal to begin. "This is Jay Rawlings coming to you from the Great Wall of China this morning. We have spent the last three weeks travelling throughout this land, praising and worshipping the Lord, and loving the people. Truly the Lord has done great things whereof we are glad. It was over ten years ago now that the Lord spoke to Meridel about this very trip. What did He say, darling?" Jay leaned the mike in my direction.

"China was firmly closed in 1969 when the Lord gave me the first vision in which we were standing on the Great Wall of China just as we are today, giving a prophetic word of release out over the nation. He spoke to us very specifically concerning the 24th day of September, 1979. This tour was planned by the Chinese authorities months ago and we had no control over where we would be and when, but here we are on the Great Wall today, September 24. We feel that this is a time of new beginnings for China. We have a wonderful group of people with us from many different backgrounds and professions, who have come to praise and to bless China."

Jay continued, "We covet your prayers, and ask that you will remember this nation before God in prayer. Pray that He will bless His Chinese peoples mightily in this hour. We see such a simplicity and openness among them. They have responded very warmly to any kindness and have loved our singing. In fact, the response has been tremendous and we praise God for the privilege to be here in China." Then Jay handed the mike to me and said, "I believe the Lord has given you a prophetic word, Meridel."

In obedience I stood, eyes closed, with raised hands, praying out in a Chinese tongue I had never learned. The following word came: "For the Lord says unto you, 'O Great Land of Sinim, I shall rule you, and you shall be ruled from on High,' says the Lord. 'I will make a way, and you will truly come up unto My land, and you will learn of Me, and you will bow before Me.' And the Lord says unto you, 'I release your peoples, I take off of them the spirit of heaviness, and I will give unto them the spirit of joy. I speak life and they shall live, and they shall praise Me from every hole, and from every rock and every field,' says the Lord.

"For the heart of the King is in the hand of the Lord and He turns it whithersoever way He will. And this day the Lord your God opens the gates, and the flood of the love of thy God shall cover you from the North to the South and the East to the West."

This prophetic word was given during the filming of our television program, on the Great Wall, and has been aired at least twice coast-to-coast in Canada on "100 Huntley Street."

Afterward we strolled about the Wall before returning to the train. Jay and I were immediately surrounded by four tour guides, one of them our own. "Come quickly with us, we have a bus waiting..." one said. We followed obediently, not realizing what they wanted nor where they were taking us. We got into the small bus. They gave the driver instructions to drive five minutes down the road. Consternation filled my mind. "What are they going to do with us," I wondered. The bus came to an abrupt stop at the edge of the road, completely out of sight of anybody. The two women guides said almost the same thing in unison, "Tell us all you know about God...."

Jay and I were surprised by their intense sincerity. "What do you want to know?" Jay asked.

"How do you know Him like you do?" came the rapid-fire reply. For five short minutes we did our best to answer one searching question after the other.

"Here," I said, "take my Bible and read it for yourself!" I handed it to one of the girls. "Read all of it," I instructed.

Our guide said, "Quick, it's time to get back to the train now." They ordered the driver to return us to the train, and just as quickly as we had been picked up, we were dropped off on the side of the road, exactly opposite our train car, minus my Bible. China and her people who are so unassuming, yet sensitive and loving, have a way of winning one's heart. Lunches had been packed for the next leg of our excursion and we devoured them as we sat in the autumn countryside at the Ming Tombs.

Late that afternoon we returned to Beijing, very tired but genuinely enriched from the day's experiences. A message at the hotel said, "Ed called." Jay rang his number, "Ed, how are you?"

"Hi, Jay, just fine. Can I drop by later tonight? There are some things I'd like to talk to you about."

"Sure, Ed," Jay responded, "is nine o'clock okay?"

"Great, see you then." He hung up.

We were in the middle of packing for our early morning departure when Ed arrived, with the film tucked under his arm.

"Here," Jay said, moving a pile of clothes, "sit down, make yourself comfortable. Tell us, how did it go?"

Ed's cheeks were rosy red from the cool night air, and his eyes were bright with a sense of accomplishment as he spoke. "Well, the first thing I did, was to present the film to the faculty of the Peking University for a special showing. They all viewed it and approved of my showing it to the student body. 'It is good educational material,' they said. It wasn't difficult at all. Then Pamela took the film to her faculty at the Normal School. They screened and approved it. She in turn was given full permission to show it to the entire student body. Thanks so much for bringing it, Jay. I needed to see it as much as my students did," he confessed.

"Oh, you are most welcome!" Jay said. "Say, I still have these *Jerusalem Post*s and they are taking up needed space in my suitcase. Would you be interested in reading them Ed?"

"So much for Chinese-Israeli relations," Ed said, rolling them together, and putting them inside of his jacket. "I think it's very interesting that you were the person to premiere 'The Last Generation' in Beijing. The Lord has a good sense of humor, don't you think?" Jay grinned at his fellow Canadian.

"I guess I'm not exactly a Zionist," he blushed. "When do you go back to Jerusalem?" Ed asked.

"In about three weeks. Our boys are there with my parents. You are welcome to come and visit us any time. You know that, don't you?"

"Thanks..." he paused. "Jay, there is one thing, I wonder if you could help me with?"

"What's that?"

"Could you send me some Bibles?"

"Sure Ed, but what do you want them for?"

"Well," his reply was straightforward, "one of my students is the son of the former Bishop of Foochow and he has never seen a Bible. It is perfectly legitimate for us to use them in the English literature class."

"Wonderful, we'll do all that we can to help you. Just be sure to look us up when you come to Israel."

"Well, for the first time in my life, I can see it as a possibility. It's been good meeting you. Here is my address. Send the 'reading materials' as quickly as you can okay? Thanks Jay!"

"Shalom."

"Give our thanks to Pam too, Ed! And keep up the good work! Shalom."

September 24 had indeed been a great day!

THE PEOPLE'S REPUBLIC OF CHINA

Jay Rawlings
U.S.A.

20
The Aliyah Van

"The great ingathering, the Aliyah, remains the ultimate mission of our generation."

Prime Minister Begin on the eve of Israel's 35th birthday (1983)

The "Aliyah Van" is a brainchild of the World Zionist Organization in Jerusalem. With a small crew of Israelis the "Aliyah Van" travelled through ten southern states in the U.S.A. Current films and exhibits were used to spark interest in Israel amongst the smaller American Jewish communities. Governors, mayors, synagogue leaders and churchmen were also visited. Israel's projected aim for the 80's is to see 100,000 North American Jews make "aliyah" or come up to live in Israel. The "van" was a part of this drive.

Although our travels had been extensive in the past, we had spent very little time in North America. Jay was asked by "100 Huntley Street" to come for a ten-month period specifically for the purpose of promoting the film "Apples of Gold." He was delighted at this opportunity to visit Christian and Jewish communities as a voice for Israel. Before leaving Jerusalem, Jay was also invited to join the "Aliyah Van" as it made its way across the southern U.S.A. Their first meeting was arranged for the fall in North Carolina.

It was an Indian summer. Warm golden rays filtered down through large spreading maple trees. The taxi drove onto Duke University campus past lawns blanketed with the rust and golds of autumn leaves. The driver swung his vehicle into the large circular courtyard up to the middle of the campus. Jay unloaded his suitcase in front of a spired gray stone church, outlined with ivy which clung tenaciously to its sides. Students casually strolled past, carefree in sneakers, absorbed in the rock music blaring from pocket transistors. No one paid any attention to the bearded Canadian in shirt and tie. Rich throbbing tones from a pipe organ flowed out from the church.

Not knowing exactly where to meet the "Aliyah Van," Jay decided to walk in the direction of the organ music. In the vestibule of the church a lady sat selling tickets for the organ recital in progress. Leaning over, Jay whispered, "Excuse me, do you know where the Hillel group is meeting today?" Without a moment's hesitation she answered, "Oh, it's down in the basement here. Go out and around to the back and you'll find the door leading down to the conference rooms."

Opening the door bearing the sign, "Interfaith Meeting Room," Jay poked his head inside. "Hi Jay," shouted Charlie, a familiar face from Jerusalem. Another fellow was piling literature on tables. "Come on and meet Bobby. This is Jay, also from Jerusalem."

"How has it been going so far?" Jay asked.

"Well," Charlie began, "we've visited Washington and Richmond so far, and the response has been good."

"You guys have just arrived too, eh?" Jay observed the stacks of books and information sheets, half-opened suitcases and coats slung on a sofa.

"Yes, we did, but it's all set," said Bobby. "We have arranged a showing of 'Apples of Gold' tonight."

At eight p.m. an interesting group of fifty Jewish and five Muslim students arrived, including an Iraqi and an Iranian, whose countries were at war with each other. In spite of the break in diplomatic relations between their nations, they were united by one thing—hatred for Israel. However, because of the apathy of the Jewish students, no heated debates began. They all sat through "Apples of Gold" looking bored and whispering. During the terrorist sequence several laughed and talked. Indignation burned in Jay. When the lights came on, he glanced at Charlie who gave him the signal to go ahead.

No one was even listening as he stood to speak, "You should be ashamed of yourselves." Jay raised his voice above the din and began again, "You should be ashamed of yourselves," he repeated. This time all eyes were focused on him. The room became quiet.

"Let it be known," Jay continued, "that in the hundreds of times I have screened this film, it was at Duke University that the audience snickered and laughed during the terrorist sequence. This is the first time it has ever happened. I'm not sure whether you laughed because you were embarrassed about Yossi's story or because you could not care less. Here you sit in North America pampered, unaware of what is actually happening in Israel. Your own people are paying a price to realize the dream of the prophets, and your response is one of disinterest. We are talking about the most important events in the world, and your own futures." All eyes were glued on him. He continued, lowering his voice, "We are fed a steady diet of violence and terror on television and in movies here in North America. People actually enjoy watching violence here because they have no personal experience of the hell that it really is. It's time to wake up! You, as young Jews in America, are a minority group and need to get your priorities right. Israel has a lot to offer you, and vice versa, we need you, I challenge you to go and see for yourselves."

The two Israelis were a little taken aback at his very direct speech, but it seemed to clear the air and the students opened up afterward. The evening took a turn for the better. Over bagels, lox and coffee, the young people entered into dynamic discussions.

By midnight Charlie, Bobby and Jay were settled into a very ordinary motel in downtown Durham. They booked adjoining rooms with Bobby and Jay sharing a room. Early the following morning, Bobby, an observant Jew, was up at the first sign of light to say his prayers. Quietly he put on his tallit or prayer shawl and his tefillin, which are leather pouches with Scriptures inside, worn on the forehead and left arm next to the heart.

Bobby opened the door to the balcony, onto a very foggy morning. "Jay," he whispered, "could you come and help me find which way is 'East'?" It was so foggy they couldn't even discern a shadow of the sun. A directional judgment was made, and Bobby began his prayers facing east, in the direction of Jerusalem. Meanwhile Jay carried on with his Bible reading and prayer.

Just as Bobby was finishing his prayers, the telephone rang. It was Charlie. "Quick, turn on the T.V. There is a program on called '700 Club' with something about Israel!"

"Come join us!" Jay said, as he quickly put down the receiver and switched on the T.V. just in time to hear Pat Robertson speaking. "Something unusual happened in Israel, called the Christian Embassy, and it was opened in Jerusaelm, and that had a great deal of significance. The Jerusalem people were saying, 'Well, Jerusalem is our capital.' The United States and several other countries refuse to recognize Jerusalem as the capital, with embassies, as it were, in Tel Aviv, and consulate offices in Jerusalem. It was a very significant thing, diplomatically, if you will, that a large group of Christians opened an embassy right in Jerusalem, saying, 'This indeed is the capital city of Israel.' Let's go right now to an overview that Peter Darg did a few months ago about the Christian Embassy."

A fanfare of trumpets sounded: Merv and Merla Watson came on the screen singing, "Blessed be the Lord God of Israel, Who only doeth wondrous things...."

Jay explained, "That's the Watsons who are responsible for the music and choreography of the Christian Celebration of the Feast of Tabernacles." Then the camera flashed to a man giving a speech, "and that's Jan Willem van der Hoeven...." "Sh...." The Israelis were fascinated.

"Dear Mr. Kollek, we are here from many different nations of the earth representing millions of Christian believers who would like to have been here with us at this time. These last weeks must not have been very easy for you, seeing the embassies one after the other leave this city for which you have worked so hard. For the first time in years Jerusalem is an open city where all religions can conduct their affairs in freedom. Today as we open the International Christian Embassy, because we believe in the God of Israel and the promises in His book, the Bible, we will remain in this city and pray for it's peace and work for it's good, knowing that in the end all will be well.

"Now, you may wonder who the ambassador is going to be. I wonder if all the enemies of Israel, with their oil weapons and the other weapons they used to push the last eight ambassadors out of the city, would have re-thought their strategy if they had realized how many would be coming back. All of us are going to represent this embassy. Here are your ambassadors. [The camera panned the enthusiastic crowds applauding gleefully.] I don't think that Jerusalem has ever had so many Christian ambassadors who will go back to their different nations, whose flags you see here, to tell the story that Israel has a right to live, because the future of Israel is the future of the world and mankind."

Again a fanfare of trumpets as the first flag, that of Australia, was planted, followed by the British Isles. "Hey, that's Meridel, planting the Canadian flag." Jay gave them a running commentary. As she presented the flag she said: "It is my privilege to speak on behalf of the millions of Christians in Canada who recognize God's promise to His people in this land of Israel and for a unified Jerusalem."

With the presentation of every flag there was a fanfare of trumpets. "There's the Stars and Stripes, Charlie." "Sh... sh... Jay...." Dr. Larry Samuels representing the U.S.A.

said: "It is a great privilege to speak on behalf of millions of people in our nation who have cried out that they might have a voice beyond that of our government or our national church bodies in this undivided city of Jerusalem." [applause]

Jay's face flashed on the screen. "I'm just going to read a couple of the multitude of telegrams that we have received from all over the world.

> 'Washington D.C. U.S.A.
> Congratulations to the organizing committee and Christians behind this Godly effort.
> Roger V. Jepsen
> United States Senator
> IOWA
>
> Oisterwijk, The Netherlands
> Re: International Christian Embassy express solidarity with fellow Christians seeking Christian support for unified Jerusalem STOP Shall continue efforts within Roman Catholic Church
> Alting Vongeusau.' "

Again a fanfare of trumpets and Mayor Kollek of Jerusalem was speaking: "Well, friends, this is one of the most moving ceremonies I have ever attended. Thank you all for coming here and for doing this. This was your idea, it came from the bottom of your hearts, it was a pure idealistic idea which was carried out here today and supported by the millions behind you all over the world.

"Jerusalem has been strong only because of its spiritual values, otherwise it would be a city like any other. There is only one Jerusalem—yours and ours. What you have done today weighs against all the various embassies that have left. They, after all, represented only governments and you represent the people.

"Sustain your intentions, work at it hard, as we are trying to work at it hard. Make this not only a one-time ceremony of today, but a living thing that will spread the word of one united Jerusalem open to all religions, to all groups, as it never has been before. Make this your home whenever you are here. It will be your home and will be our most honored, treasured and respected representation in this city. Thank you very much."

The T.V. studio audience applauded as the film clip ended. Charlie switched off the T.V. "How many people does this program reach?" he asked.

"Conservatively in the millions, every day," Jay said.

"Well, I'm amazed to see the depth of understanding concerning Israel." He was noticeably impressed.

"It's happening at long last," Jay concluded. "This has been the hope of many of us for years. Christians are becoming alerted worldwide to the vital importance of standing with Israel. You'll have to drop in and see the folks at the Embassy when you return to Jerusalem."

"Were you involved in that too, Jay?"

"Yes, Meridel and I were invited to be on the planning committee for the first large Christian Celebration of the Feast of Tabernacles. The inspiration to open the Embassy came to Jan Willem van der Hoeven after all the embassies pulled out of Jerusalem. We encouraged the idea and were co-founders of the Embassy along with many other very dedicated Christians in Jerusalem."

Several months later *The Jerusalem Post* carried an article about the Aliyah Van entitled, "On the Road to Zionism":

> They were unofficially joined during their treks through Georgia and Texas by Reverend Jay Rawlings, a Christian activist living in Jerusalem, who made such pro-Israel, anti-P.L.O. and anti-Palestinian declarations before his audiences that the two emissaries almost felt embarrassed by his fervor. [End of quote.]

21
Hunters

. . . and afterwards will I send for many hunters, and they shall hunt them from every mountain and from every hill, and out of the clefts of the rocks.

Jeremiah 16:16b

Throughout history the Jewish people have had to contend with a host of enemies that have sought their destruction. Some of these "hunters" from ancient times to the present, include the Amalekites, Pharaoh of Egypt, Haman of Babylon, the Assyrians, the Romans, the Crusaders, the Inquisitors of Spain, the pogroms of 19th Century Russia and Eastern Europe, the Nazis and, currently, the hostile Arab States and the USSR.

One of the most well known additions to this ignominious list is the PLO, or Palestine Liberation Organization. In this chapter we will focus on some of the background information of this well equipped, heavily financed organization whose stated objectives are the liquidation of the modern state of Israel and the genocide of its people.

On the surface, the struggle appears nationalistic but the real issues are spiritual. To understand, one must hearken back to the Biblical events of two peoples, Arab and Jew, both descendants of Abraham claiming the same land . . . Palestine or Israel.

The History of Palestine

The term Palestine originally applied to the territory of

Israel's foes, the Philistines. This area was generally located on the coastal plains of the south-eastern end of the Mediterranean Sea, north of Gaza and Egypt. The size of the area varied according to historical developments in the vicinity. Originally the Philistines were believed to have migrated from Egypt. By the second century A.D., Roman politics bore a familiar ring to our present day. They gave the name "Palestina" to the area which entered history as the sovereign homeland of the Jewish nation more than 3,000 years ago. Their purpose was to eradicate the Jews' link to the land. Some twenty centuries later, the League of Nations Mandate coined the term "Palestinian" to apply to all peoples, Jews, Christians and Muslims alike, who lived in a large area that today is made up of Israel, Jordan and parts of Iraq. From 1917, with Britain as a mandatory power, Palestine was partitioned and over 77% became the Kingdom of Jordan, while 23% west of the River Jordan went to the Jews. In 1946 the establishment of the independent Palestinian state of Transjordan, later renamed "The Hashemite Kingdom of Jordan" meant the realization of the Palestinian Arab's right of self-determination in the greater part of Palestine.

In 1947 the UN sought to settle the ensuing conflict by another partition, this time of western Palestine, into Jewish and Arab states. Although the Jews were awarded the smallest territory possible, they accepted the resolution, hoping this compromise would lead to a peaceful solution of this dispute. The Arabs rejected the UN plan and attacked Israel on May 15, 1948. The regular armies of Egypt, Transjordan, Iraq, Syria, and Lebanon invaded. Azzam Pasha, Secretary-General of the Arab League proclaimed in Cairo: "This will be a war of extermination and a momentous massacre . . ."

By mid-1948 two independent sovereign states existed in the area once known as Palestine: the Arab-Palestinian state of Jordan in eastern Palestine and the Jewish Palestinian state of Israel in western Palestine. For this very reason another Arab Palestinian state was not established in western Palestine, the so-called "West Bank", or Biblical Judea and Samaria, during the 19 years it was controlled by Jordan from 1948 to 1967. A glance at the map will show that the establishment of a potentially hostile third state within the narrow 50 mile wide area between the Mediterranean Sea and the Jordan River would be a constant threat to Israel's security.

After 1948, over 400,000 Palestinian Arabs from Judea and Samaria chose to move to Jordan. Today Jordan's population, even without the western area it lost in its abortive attack on Israel in 1967, is still composed mostly of Arabs of west Palestinian origin. The rest of the Arabs are of east Palestinian origin. As Jordan's King Hussein said in an interview for the Paris-based An-Nahar al-Arabi w'al-Douli, on 26 December 1981, "The truth is that Jordan is Palestine and Palestine is Jordan."

According to scripture, Judea and Samaria belong to Israel. It is not just a coincidence that Jeremiah prophesied to the Jewish people,

> "Thou shalt yet plant vines upon the mountains of Samaria: the planters shall plant, and shall eat them as common things. For there shall be a day, that the watchmen upon the mount Ephraim shall cry, Arise ye, and let us go up to Zion unto the Lord our God."[1]

He goes on to describe how He is bringing His people home from the four corners of the earth.

Jeremiah also prophesied over Judah (the name Jew is derived from Judah), "Thus saith the Lord of hosts, the God of Israel: As yet they shall use this speech (Hebrew) in the land of Judah and in the cities thereof, when I shall bring again their captivity."[2]

PLO — "The Destroyers"

Within the Muslim world the PLO have been referred to in

---

[1] Jeremiah 31:5, 6

[2] Jeremiah 31:23

Arabic as the "muharabeen" or the destroyers. This title evolved as the shortened form of the descriptive phrase "the destroyers of the Zionist entity". However, recent events in Lebanon have clearly shown that their name has a grim prophetic application to themselves. For example, in Beirut thousands of innocent Lebanese and Palestinians have been killed or maimed by the Palestinian "revolution" carried out in conjunction with the Soviet-backed Syrian occupation force.

The Palestinian Liberation Organization officially came into being on May 22, 1964, in the midst of political unrest and instability in the Arab world. It has the distinction of pioneering modern terrorism. On a summer night in 1964, three years before the Six Day War, Yasser Arafat forded the River Jordan, climbed a hill near Nablus, fired one shot from his pistol, and declared: "The Jihad or holy war has begun."

Arafat was born in Gaza in 1929, his birth was registered with the Egyptian Ministry of the Interior. His full name reveals his kinship to the former Grand Mufti of Jerusalem, Haj Amin el-Husseini. For years during the British Mandate this devoutly irreligious man was the spiritual leader of Jerusalem's Muslims. He is well known for collaborating with the Nazis. Haj Amin played host to the leaders of Hitler's Germany on his own villa in Berlin. He did everything he could to secure a German victory. Fully aware of the "Final Solution", he did his best to see that none of its intended victims were diverted to Palestine on their way to Himmler's gas chambers. In 1943, he personally intervened with Reich Foreign Minister Ribbentrop to prevent the emigration of 4,000 Jewish children from Bulgaria to Palestine.[3]

Arafat threatened death to any Arab journalist who mentioned his blood relationship to Haj Amin, the Grand Mufti. "I am the Palestine people," he said, "and the Palestinian people are me."[4]

---

[3] Larry Collins and Dominique LaPierre, O Jerusalem. Simon and Shuster, 1972, pp. 43–44.

[4] Source unknown.

> "Don't rejoice, Philistines, that the king who smote you is dead. That rod is broken, yes; but his son will be a greater scourge to you than his father ever was! From the snake will be born an adder, a fiery serpent to *destroy you!* I will shepherd the poor of my people. They shall graze in my pasture! The needy shall lie down in peace. But as for you, I will wipe you out with famine and the sword. Weep, Philistine cities, you are doomed. All your nation is doomed. For a perfectly trained army is coming down from the north against you. What then shall we tell the reporters? Tell them that the Lord has founded Jerusalem and is determined that the poor of his people will find a refuge within her walls."[5]

In 1951 Arafat became a student of engineering at the University of Cairo. He was a junior officer in the Egyptian army in 1951 during the Suez crisis. From the mid-50's on, his energies were spent touring the Palestine diaspora, preaching his gospel of "liberation" and recruiting members for his organization, Fatah. The title, Fatah, is the reversed initials, in Arabic, for Movement for the Liberation of Palestine, Harakat, al-Tahrir al-Watani al-Filistini (watani = national). Fatah itself means conquest.

Fatah delegates to the Palestine National Congress in Cairo met the world's press for the first time in June 1965. They expressed their policy with startling directness, "To entangle the Arab nations in war with Israel."[6]

In 1965, President Nasser of Egypt said, "The Palestinians are useful to the Arab States as they are, we will always see that they do not become too powerful. Can you imagine yet another nation on the shores of the eastern Mediterranean."

The fundamental commitment of the Arabs is to the doc-

---

[5] Isaiah 14:29–32 The Living Bible.

[6] John Laffin, The PLO Connections, Corgi Books, 1982, p. 34.

trine of pan-Arabism, not Palestinian self-determination. Arab animosity to Israel they say is the result of Israeli occupation of Arab land, not Palestinian. Between 1948 and 1967 Palestinian refugees languished in refugee camps ignored by the great mass of Arabs and unnoticed by the rest of the world. Only after Israel occupied the West Bank, Judea and Samaria, in 1967 did the Arabs show concern for the Palestinian people and for their welfare.

The Palestinian People and the PLO

From the outset it is absolutely essential to draw some distinctions between the Palestinian people and the PLO terrorist organization.

With the expulsion of the PLO from Beirut and from nearly all of southern Lebanon, some courageous Palestinians are now willing to express their true feelings toward the PLO, and their supporters. Mustafa Dudein, head of the Palestinian Village League on the West Bank, said in an interview with the Jerusalem Post on May 24, 1983, "We do not believe any Arab State wants to fight for the Palestinian cause. The PLO are not one body. They are 10 different factions with 10 different loyalties. Each one belongs to a different Arab regime. At the same time the Palestinian covenant calls for the demolition of the Israeli state and I don't think any wise man in the world can accept such an idea now."[7]

Together, during the war in Lebanon in July 1982, Jay, and Irving Boren, an industrialist from California, carried out personal interviews in Lebanon with Palestinian refugees and former PLO terrorists. These people, who had been silenced for years, freely expressed their repulsion at the motives and modus operandi of the PLO. For many now their hope is to live in peace with the Lebanese and Israelis. Through these interviews it was made painfully clear that the PLO and their widely quoted leaders do not accurately represent the true

---

[7] Mustafa Dudein, the Jerusalem Post, May 24, 1983.

feelings and aspirations of the Palestinian people. A people, held as hostages for 35 years in the refugee camps and intimidated by the terror tactics of the PLO, who have as a result been given the dubious reputation as a bunch of thugs and terrorists. Hence the world tends to lump the PLO and the Palestinian people together as one group. This is unfair to the majority of diligent peace-loving Palestinians. In western Galilee in Israel for example, Jewish and Arab farmers live together in peace, harmony, and productivity, and have done so for many years. Unfortunately this is not reported in the world press.

One of the men of the region making "good news" is Ibrihim Simaan, a local Baptist minister who has worked tirelessly bringing wounded Lebanese and their families to the Rambam Hospital in Haifa for treatment and social assistance. His work spans much of the war in Lebanon. He said to us during our interviews:

"I'm proud to be a Palestinian, but as proud to be an Israeli, and as proud to be a Christian. All right, those are three ingredients that form up some of my personality. This now brings me to the answer to a question you asked. I do this kind of work as a kind of self-therapy, because this war is really going on within me. And I could not decide where my loyalties are, but at last I made my decision: my loyalty is to my God. And God is the Father of all humanity and to deserve life we must look for what is common for all people and not for what divides us up. Therefore part of my ministry is not just providing financial aid for artificial limbs or a bite to eat, sometimes all that is needed is a smile and the ability to return to this people the ability to smile."

The Palestinian people have never participated in choosing the leaders of the PLO or in the formulation of its policy. There is an appointed PLO legislature or council of 100 members which includes people from many walks of life, but it meets only twice a year, and its members dare not form groups or factions which might be seen as hostile to the cabinet or executive committee. The importance of the council is its mere existence, it helps the Arab world recognize the PLO as the only so-called legitimate representative of the Arab Palestinians. At times the PLO has consisted of up to 40 organizations backed by various Arab regimes. It is this pan-Arab recognition which gives the PLO its impressive international status. This status was ratified at the Rabat Summit in 1974 when the PLO became the twenty-third member of the Arab League and was recognized as the "sole legitimate representative" of the Palestinian people. In fact, the Palestinian people were never asked to vote or to pass a referendum on the matter, the basis of any democratic society. As a result of this "self-appointed" status, most western democracies, including the U.S.A., will not recognize the PLO in the negotiation procedures of the Middle East peace initiatives. It is essential to stress that the PLO was not created by the demand of the Palestinian people. The PLO created itself and claims to represent the Palestinian Arabs who live in the territory of the British mandate region called Palestine which comprise the territory of both the present day state of Israel, including the region of Judea and Samaria known as the West Bank, and the Hashemite Kingdom of Jordan. The demographic spread of these Palestinians is very interesting, 70% live in Jordan and Israel, while 24% live in other Arabic states and 6% live outside the Middle East.

The majority of Palestinians are Jordanian citizens whom the PLO does not represent, in spite of its own claims to the contrary. In fact, in 1970 King Hussein of Jordan forcibly expelled and killed thousands of Palestinians during the Black September incident over the issue of Jordanian sovereignty and PLO anarchy. Thus the majority of Palestinians who remained in Jordan have full Jordanian citizenship. To date no effort has been made to sound out public opinion among them as to their real hopes and aspirations. Similarly, most Palestinians that Jay spoke to in Southern Lebanon had absolutely no desire to go and live in a Palestinian state in the West

Bank (see Chapter 43 for further details). However, this position is not acceptable to the PLO leadership whose declared position and overriding objectives remain unchanged, "the absolute and final elimination of the state of Israel."

The Palestinian Covenant

> "They have taken crafty counsel against thy people and consulted against thy hidden ones. They have said, Come and let us cut them off from being a nation; that the name of Israel may be no more in remembrance. For they have consulted together with one consent: they are confederate against thee."[8]

The Palestinian national covenant contains the PLO's strategy and fundamental aims. It was first drawn up in 1964 and later revised in 1969 after the Fatah faction takeover of the PLO. It contains some 33 articles, a few of which are quoted here.

> Article 9: "Armed struggle is the only way to liberate Palestine and is therefore a strategy and not tactics."
>
> Article 15: "The liberation of Palestine, from an Arab viewpoint, is a national duty to repulse the Zionist, imperialist invasion from the great Arab homeland and to purge the Zionist presence from Palestine."
>
> Article 16: "Jews who are living permanently in Palestine until the beginning of the Zionist invasion (1948) will be considered Palestinians."
>
> Article 19: "The partitioning of Palestine in 1947 and the establishment of Israel is fundamentally null and void, whatever time has elapsed."
>
> Article 20: "The Balfour Declaration of 1917, the Mandate Document, and what has been based upon them are considered null and void."

---

[8] Psalm 83:3–6.

> Article 22: "Zionism is a political movement organically related to world imperialism and hostile to all movements of liberation and progress in the world. It is a racist and fanatical movement in its formation: aggressive, expansionist and colonialist in its aims."[9]

The Islamic Revolution

To comprehend the origins of the "Palestinian covenant", one must look carefully at the role the PLO has assumed in the pan-Arab scheme of international politics.

Recent events in the Muslim world have startled even the most sanguine of international observers. The rapid overthrow of Iran under the fundamentalist Muslim leader Ayatolla Khomeini has sent shock waves into the courts of less observant Arab leaders. In fact, the entire Arab world is in ferment over tensions that are developing between extremist Muslim factions and conservative leadership groups. The word Islam means "submission" to the will of Allah and Muslim fundamentalists agree that the teachings of Mohammed have superceded Judaism and Christianity. They believe that Islam is a superior socio-religious system that is destined to rule and dominate the entire world. The recent rise of the oil rich Arab states to the center of the global economy serves to confirm this belief.

The creation and growth of a Jewish State in the heartland of the Islamic region undermines basic Muslim theology. To a devout follower of Mohammed this can never be accepted or tolerated. Thus the PLO is a convenient tool to support and encourage for the destruction of this unacceptable "Zionist entity". Such rationale explains the transfer of enormous sums of petro-dollars to the PLO from Saudi Arabia, Libya and Iran. One of Khomeini's first acts in power was to publi-

---

[9] Leila S. Kadi ed., PLO Organization Research Center Beirut, December 1969, pp. 137–141.

cally thank the PLO for its part in the Iranian revolution and to transfer ten million dollars from the Central Bank in Teheran to the PLO in Beirut. In May of 1979 an Arabic Islamic conference in Morocco was held to discuss the liberation of Jerusalem. A secret plan was set up whereby oil was to be used as a weapon and means of pressure. Jerusalem must no longer remain in the hands of the "infidel" Jews they said. No sacrifice was too great. When the conference was dismissed the delegates, including the PLO, called to each other "until next year in Jerusalem".[10]

The ancient Islamic concept of a "jihad" or holy war is regularly used to flame Arab passions to "liberate all of the Israeli occupied territories" and the old city of Jerusalem. The PLO have responded with regular acts of terror and violence in Israel, many times using teenagers who have been told that should they die in this "holy war" to liberate Jerusalem they will go immediately to paradise. In fact this jihad concept is used by Khomeini in the Iran-Iraq war where between 300,000 and 400,000 young men and boys have died in a series of horrific battles known as the "War for the Liberation of Jerusalem".

Yasser Arafat repeats the teaching tirelessly. The way to paradise, he says, lies through Jerusalem and if a young man dies striving for the return of the eastern part of the city to Arab hands he will be a martyr among martyrs.[11] It is evident that the Islamic revolution serves to regularly inject new surges of idealistic fervor into the veins of the PLO in its desire to rid the Middle East of the "infidels" and to have Islam embraced on a world wide scale.

Finances

The PLO is a deluxe terror group. Uniquely, it operates from office blocks with a paid staff working regular hours,

---

[10] Marius Baar, The Unholy War, Thomas Nelson Publishers, Nashville: 1980, p. 139.

[11] Israel Information Center, P.O. Box 13010, Jerusalem, May 1978.

taking annual holidays and receiving PLO pensions. Because of the extensive aid it receives from the Arab States and from the Soviet Union, it is strong politically and financially.

At the Baghdad Summit of November 1978, it was decided that a number of Arab states would contribute a total of $250 million annually to the PLO and another $150 million to a joint Jordanian-PLO fund designed to "reinforce the steadfastness" of the inhabitants of Judea-Samaria and the Gaza district. Until then, the chief benefactor of the PLO had been Libya which provided it with $75 million annually, as well as special donations for "outstanding successes", such as the $5 million donated for the murder of eleven Israeli athletes at the Munich Olympics.

Extortion and protection, blackmail and hijacking, have also raised large sums. A ransom demand of $5 million was paid for the release of a Lufthansa aircraft hijacked in Yemen in February 1977 with 190 passengers and crew. Twenty-five million dollars were paid for the release of the hostages held at the OPEC headquarters in Vienna in December 1975.

Drug smuggling has also been used to raise money. In June 1977 the Guardian newspaper of London reported that Interpol had uncovered a PLO drug smuggling ring operating in Europe and the Middle East. Its members were believed to have accumulated some $2 million in profits which were used for the purchase of arms. Reports of embezzlement have also come to public attention. On October 30, 1976, Radio Beirut reported that some 1.5 to 2 billion Lebanese pounds had been transferred to the private bank accounts of several PLO leaders.[12]

Saudi Arabia is the largest financial backer. Between 1978 and 1982, the Saudis poured some $320 million petro-dollars into PLO coffers. Following a meeting in Ryadh in March 1982 between Yasser Arafat and King Fahd, the Saudis agreed to grant the PLO an additional $250 million for arms purchases.

---

[12] Ibid., Nov. 1979.

The budget is estimated at $1 million per day, used mainly for salaries and expenses for its estimated 15,000 members. Significant amounts went into the pockets of the PLO commanders, who controlled the cash flow and channelled it into such private investments as gold and drug smuggling, "for the sake of the Palestinian revolution".

Schools of Terror

The PLO used its years in Lebanon to build up a network of training and logistic installations usually in and around Palestinian refugee camps. Their assumption was that the close proximity to civilian populations would give them immunity from attack or retaliation by Lebanese or Israelis. This became known as the "human shield" tactic. There were four main training camps for foreign terrorists in Lebanon: Shatilla, Burj el Burajneh, Shabriha, and Damour. A Nazi-type organization, "Turkish Gray Wolves" was trained in Damour. This is the group to which Agca, who attempted to assassinate the Pope, belonged. Only 200 yards down the street from where the Turks trained, were the offices of an American terrorist group. Damour's 25,000 Christian inhabitants were driven out in January 1976.

Psychologists with specialized knowledge of the "fear factor" were brought in. Trainees are taught that the greatest terror can be inflicted on adults by threats, either explicit or implicit, against children. Such threats have been made many times against those Israeli Arabs who have not been ready enough to help the PLO with safe houses, money and information. The principles come straight from the KGB manual on treatment of political prisoners.

Since 1966 these terrorist schools have proliferated, spreading to Syria, Iraq, Yemen, Egypt, Libya, Algeria, Kuwait, Uganda, the Soviet Union, East Germany, Czechoslovakia, Bulgaria and Yugoslavia. Such centers have spawned "specialists" in terror tactics who have been used to train others from such countries as Bangladesh, Sri Lanka, Pakistan, Abu

Dubai, Algeria, India, Mauritania, Morocco, Niger, Nigeria, Saudi Arabia, Somalia, Sudan, Tunisia and Turkey. Many sought to escape poverty enticed by promises of wealth and glory. The salaries offered, between $80 to $300 per month, sounded like fortunes to these mostly impoverished young men.

Propaganda

The PLO's propaganda argument is that terror was the last resort of a desperate, homeless people and hence a legitimate form of political expression. The concept blurred the world's distinction between criminal and military action.

Unfortunately the innocent Palestinian people have been the unwitting victims of the PLO propaganda machine. The refugee problem has been maintained at the expense of the innocent Palestinians in an area where more than one million Jewish refugees have been successfully rehabilitated since 1948. Tragically, the refugee camps have been turned into breeding grounds of hate and terror from infancy to adulthood. Reaching maturity with only one thought in mind, the destruction of Israel, has led many fine young Palestinian men to their deaths, taking innocent Jewish citizens with them. These young men could have been given educational and beneficial alternatives by careful investment of Arab petrodollars, but according to the PLO party line such benevolence would not advance the Palestinian revolution.

The "conspiracy of silence" in the media began about four years after the PLO entered Beirut. Lebanese president, Suleiman Franjieh, made an historic blunder in 1974 when he paved the way for Arafat's tragic-comic show at the podium of the United Nations General Assembly. The arch terrorist was turned into an international figure. Until this point people had no problem recognizing terrorism. After Arafat appeared at the U.N. a change occurred. The U.N. became a theater rather than a debating chamber. Hundreds of journalists wanted to interview PLO chiefs and record their views for radio and press and television. Crowned with victory and world-wide prestige, he returned to Beirut as his capital, and let loose his armed gangs.

The PLO has cultivated a dual image, by saying different things to different people. It has acquired a reputation for being both radical and moderate, depending upon the audience addressed. To the West, it makes moderate sounding statements that are accepted at face value and featured prominently in the media. Arafat engages professional speechwriters, especially when he is to appear before a Western audience. In an NBC interview February 8, 1976, Arafat said, "We are not against civilians, we are doing our best to avoid civilians." This repetition of the message of moderation has had a greater impact than the PLO's attacks, which in fact have been almost entirely against civilian targets. To fellow Arabs, PLO leaders have always spoken in the most extreme and uncompromising terms, in full accord with the "Palestinian National Covenant". It spells out the PLO's central objective of liquidating the State of Israel, and has been reaffirmed at every official PLO enclave since 1964.

The PLO propagandists have achieved a degree of professionalism unequalled in the 20th Century and in their exploitation of the Christian world, they have used the significant Vatican anti-Israel lobby. Early in the 1970's the PLO worked to win the Christian churches of the U.S.A. to its cause. Almost unnoticed, a growing number of churches began to focus attention on the PLO. The trend was reinforced by debate over Andrew Young's unauthorized contact with a representative of the PLO when Young was U.N. Ambassador, an action that cost Young his job.

The National Council of Churches is an organization representing 31 Protestant and orthodox denominations. It made 1979–80 a "focus of study" year as requested by the PLO literature they had received. The Council's executive commended Ambassador Young for talking with the PLO representative.

The Presbyterian Church in the U.S.A. hosted several Palestinian speakers at a conference in North Carolina in July 1979. Richard Butler, director of the Middle East office of the National Council of Churches, said, "There is an increased understanding of the centrality of the Palestinian issue in the Middle East conflict. Many churches have dealt for years with the Palestinian issue as a refugee problem. Only recently have they come to recognize that the Palestinians are not just refugees, they are a people looking for a homeland." Butler's phraseology faithfully reflects PLO literature, the slogans "people looking for a homeland" and "centrality of the Palestinian issue" are the key phrases suggested by one of the public relations firms engaged by the PLO to present its case to the Americans.

Significant propaganda is issued obliquely through the United Nations Relief and Works Agency, UNRWA whose mission is to care for Palestinian refugees in Lebanon and other countries. Indirectly, but no less effectively, UNRWA was "taken over" by the PLO through Palestinians who work for UNRWA in Lebanon and to a lesser extent in other countries. The same tactics have proven extremely successful to influence the United Nations Interim Force in Lebanon, UNIFIL sent to southern Lebanon in 1976. It is interesting to note the fruit of such propaganda. Staunch supporter of the PLO cause during the "Operation Peace for Galilee" was the *West.* Israel was seen as the aggressor. More interesting perhaps was the absolute lack of support for the PLO from their friends the USSR and the Arab nations.

Media Control

A much more serious area of media control by the PLO has come to light as a result of the heavy involvement of journalists in Lebanon. Intimidation and even liquidation of foreign journalists who accurately reported PLO activities in Beirut have recently surfaced. Edouard George, a senior journalist and member of the editorial staff of the French language daily

"L'Orion du Jour", wrote an article that was published in the Hebrew daily Ma'ariv on August 27, 1982. In the article he accused the foreign and local media in Beirut of having "sold their conscience to the PLO". He exposed the story of co-operation, whether voluntary, enforced, or mercenary, between the media and the terrorist organizations, shedding light on another aspect of the PLO terror regime in Beirut. He provided facts showing how Palestinian terror had liquidated decent, courageous reporters, how they silenced the weak and the frightened with threats, and how they bribed the corrupt with petro-dollars. After checking through his files, Edouard George came up with a partial list of physical liquidations, attacks, kidnappings, explosions and sabotage that had plagued the journalistic community during the seven years of PLO rule in West Beirut. The list deals with the acts of terror perpetrated against the media until all centers of resistance had been wiped out and "PLO discipline" had been imposed on the press in West Beirut.

Between 1976 and 1981, the terrorist organizations liquidated eight foreign journalists in West Beirut including Larry Buchman, correspondent of the ABC television network; Mark Tryon of the "Free Belgium" broadcasting station; Edouard Sa'eb "Le Monde" correspondent and editor-in-chief of the Beirut daily "L'Orion du Jour"; Robert Pfeffer, correspondent for the weeklies Der Spiegel of Germany and Unita of Italy; the Italian journalists Tony Italo and Graciella DiFaco; Sean Toolan, ABC correspondent and Jean Longeau, correspondent for TV Number One in France.

Thirty six daily and weekly newspapers are published in West Beirut, most of them in Arabic and nearly all of the major world media companies have special representatives or local stringers in Beirut. "Not one of them dared to write or broadcast the truth", said Edouard George.[13] In an interview, with Aharon Dolev, Mr. George said, "I can only say that

[13] Jerusalem Press Office release, 1982.

very few will come out with a clean bill of health, and those few do not include the BBC, Radio Monte Carlo, and various British, French and even American journalists."[14]

Arms Supply

> "... no weapon that is formed against thee will prosper."[15]

The European initiative, articulated at the Venice Summit in June 1980, declared that the Palestinian people must be placed in a position to fully exercise their right of self-determination. It also asserted that the PLO will have to be associated with any peace settlement. These statements are based on the false assumptions that the Palestinian issue is the heart of the Middle East conflict. A study of the inter-Arab clashes over the last 35 years negates the concept that stability and peace in the Middle East is dependent only upon settling the Arab-Israel struggle. In fact the Middle East Casualty Audit, MECA shows that inter-Arab battles have caused some 200 times more deaths than their entire casualty total against enemy Israel since 1948.

The demand for weapons grows frighteningly with each passing year. Now the scope of the arms market is so tremendous that it overrides moral, political and intellectual arguments. The biggest and best customer is Saudi Arabia, taking about half of total Western arms shipped into the Middle East. The U.S.A. supplies much of this material, but France signed a single $2 billion arms deal in May 1980. Austria sells anti-aircraft and machine guns. Britain sold "support equipment for artillery" worth £130 million in one deal, as well as patrol boats, tanks and aircraft. Switzerland and Italy in collaboration provided Saudi Arabia with a $2.1 billion air defence system. West Germany in 1981 sold Saudi Arabia patrol boats and training ships. Also, the Germans sold Syria tanks, armoured cars and ancillary equip-

---

[14] Ibid.

[15] Isaiah 54:17.

ment. French arms deals with Iraq concluded a five year agreement with Iraq for military hardware worth $1 billion. These are just a few examples of the vast amounts of money being spent in the West. Libya, for instance, spends 4.0 billion a year. Behind all the deals was the tacit understanding that Europe will "do what it can for the PLO".[16] The world wide economic recession of the early eighties made the availability of petro-dollars through arms deals particularly appealing to the Western nations. Because the money supply was limitless, the choice was varied and the quantities incredible. Some of the consignments were shipped to Lebanon marked as tractors and bulldozer parts or medical supplies for the Red Crescent.

Finds in Lebanon

A large cache of Soviet-supplied Simenov rifles was found in Damour, each weapon bearing the swastika, known in Arabic as the Zawbahr. The Popular Party of Syria, one of whose members has been arrested for the murder of Bashir Gemayel, has a curved swastika as its emblem, but the symbol on the rifles was the rectangular swastika of Germany's Third Reich.

On July 4, 1982, the Jerusalem Post carried this article, "Israel claims it seized ammunition manufactured at a U.S. army plant in Missiouri from the PLO in Lebanon."

In a copyright story, The Kansas City Times said a large supply of machine-gun bullets was part of a 3-million round sale to Saudi Arabia in 1977. "How the ammunition reached the PLO was unclear."

Perhaps one of the strangest so-called weapons discovered in Lebanon was a "VOEST AM-50", a tunnel miner, manufactured in Austria. It was capable of mining a tunnel 3.8 meters wide and 4.0 meters high. The Beirut underground was made up of many large bunkers and tunnels as were dozens of other towns. Huge quantities of arms, ammunition and ar-

---

[16] John Laffin, The PLO Connections, Corgi Books, 1982, p. 76.

mored vehicles were stored in these tunnels. An army of 100,000 men could have been immediately equipped from the materials found.

Documents Captured June 1982[17]

Memo
Palestine National Liberation Movement
Fatah
The Martyr Kamal Aduan Battalion
To Brother Belal
To Brother Azmi

Greetings of the Revolution!

I strengthen your hands. Thus will you prove that you are heroic sons to your people and your revolution. We expect tonight the shelling of Safad and Aljaoun with heavy missiles — because of its great importance. In addition you can shell the settlements close to the border with 120 mm and 160 mm mortars, this must be carried out immediately.

Moreover, it is compulsory to dispatch joint combat patrols or detachments from your forces to lay ambushes along the border strip and deep inside the conquered land.

Yasser Arafat
18.7.81.

Excerpt from captured document:

19-7-81

Choice of Place and Timing of an Operation

1. The enemy should be struck at its weak spot, and for the enemy, *civilians* are its weak spot. *Immigration centers* of Jews to Israel should be hit and the absorption locations of new immigrants to Israel should be attacked: electrical and water

---

[17] Documents provided through the IDF Press Office, Beit Agron, Jerusalem, 1982.

installations should be hit and the places of residence or absorption of new immigrants should be set on fire.

2. The objective should be such that considerable damage will be caused to the enemy. There are places where if one hits the enemy it does not disturb it at all.
3. It is desirable to attack *tourist sites* during the tourist season. It is desirable to set fire to fuel depots, which cause considerable damage to the enemy.
4. It is necessary to act in market places and where many people congregate, especially during *holidays and vacations.* Special attention should be paid to the season and timing of the operation.
5. Steps should be taken to ensure the security of the personnel carrying out the operation.

PLO
Joint Forces Artillery

No: M/145
DATE: 21.7.81

TOP SECRET AND VERY URGENT

From: Commander of Joint Forces Artillery in the South.
To: All units.
Greetings of the Revolution!

1. The following is a list of targets and their allocation:

No.	*Target*	*Unit*	*Quantity*	*Total*
1.	Misgav Amm	Artillery Battalion 1	20	20
2.	Kiryat Shemona	El Sa'aqa	20	20
3.	She'ar Yishuv	Artillery Battalion 6	20	20
4.	Dan	"Popular Front"	20	20
5.	Kefar Yuval	"Liberation Front"	20	20

Israel	6.	Hagoshrim	"Democratic Front"	20	20
	7.	Ma'ayan Barukh	"Arab Liberation Front"	20	20
	8.	Kefar Giladi	"Liberation Front"	20	20
	9.	Metullah	Artillery Battalion 1	20	20
	10.	Nahariya	Missile Unit	20	20
	11.	Military Airfield	Artillery Battalion 3	20	20
Southern	12.	Marj Ayoun	Artillery Battalion 1	20	20
Lebanon	13.	Kle'a	Artillery Battalion 1	20	20

2. The firing will be carried out in two stages:
   A. Stage A, 1900 hrs, on 21 July 1981
   B. Stage B, 0800 hrs, on 22 July 1981

The International Connection

Since 1968 the PLO has maintained close contact with the Soviet Union in exchange for diplomatic support and arms. This symbiotic relationship has developed between the PLO and the USSR for various reasons. The Soviets recognize the advantages of supporting and aiding the world's most sophisticated terrorist organization in order to accomplish their objectives of destabilization of western governments.

The eastern bloc Marxist regimes are particularly interested in humiliating the NATO countries of Europe, in many of which the PLO has nevertheless been allowed to open offices. A PLO defector was recently quoted as saying, "We turned into a terror organization which enable the Russians to cause the blow-up of any situation. Whenever they are interested in such eruptions, all they do is come to us and give us instructions."[18]

Through the seventies the PLO became the "front" for the training and equipping of various terrorist organizations from around the world. Backed by Soviet arms and special training courses in Kiev, Moscow, and Leningrad, it has been estimated that one in ten PLO terrorists have been trained in the USSR. After 1968, the PLO and its subsidiary bodies exported terror, its targets being Western, Arab, Israeli, and Jewish targets within the Middle East and beyond. Between 1968 and

[18] New York Times, December 20, 1980.

1980, Arab terrorists committed more than 300 different attacks including bombings and shootings in 26 countries other than Israel. 813 people were killed, 1,013 were injured, and more than 90% of the 2,755 hostages were not Israelis. Targets included 40 civil airline planes, 5 passenger ships and 30 embassies or other diplomatic missions. About 40 economic targets were hit, including fuel depots and factories. More than 30 diplomats were assassinated or wounded and letter bombs were sent to numerous civilians.

The support and material aid provided the PLO by the Soviet Union is an open secret, freely spoken of at the United Nations by the UN's PLO observer. What is not as well known is the well-organized routine for the ongoing exchange of information between the PLO, especially its Fatah branch, and the USSR. There was a special telephone-tapping system in Beirut called Ekud, "Listen", and the PLO controlled the telex system. They could, therefore, tap all internal messages, including those from East Beirut. The electronic hardware which monitored the telephone and telex systems was housed close to the Soviet Embassy. The PLO controlled the West Beirut and Southern Lebanon postal services, and only the Christian enclave in East Beirut, Jounieh and the surrounding hills had independent postal services between 1975 and 1982.

By the early eighties, West Beirut had developed into a recognized headquarters of global terrorism. Over 10,000 terrorists from all over the world gravitated to this once beautiful city now lying in divided ruins and devastation. "In it any terrorist group having the Russian seal of approval, such as the IRA or Red Brigades, could obtain arms, equipment, money,forged documents, and most importantly, training, from the PLO. Evidence of the PLO's central role in international terrorism was the active participation of dozens of 'liberation organizations' at the National Council of the PLO in May 1981 in Damascus."[19]

[19] David Peleggi, Information Officer, International Christian Embassy Jerusalem, 1982.

In her recent book "The Terror Network", Claire Sterling points out the scope, degree of sophistication, and interconnection of the world terrorist infrastructure. Unfortunately, most western nations, caught up with their own internal and international problems, fail to see the serious nature of these signs. It seems only Israel has the will and physical stamina needed to curb this cancer growing within the fabric of the civilized world.

The following are underground terrorist organizations that maintain close connection with the PLO:

The Turkish Popular Liberation Army
The Eritrean Liberation Front
The Japanese Red Army
The Secret Army for the Liberation of Armenia
The Argentinian Montoneros
The Brazilian Vanguarda Popular Revolucionaria
The Chilean MIR
The Colombian Guerilla group
The Nicaraguan Sandinists, before and after they attained power
The Guatemalan MR-13
Various underground movements in San Salvador
The Uruguayan MLN, Tupamaros
The Venezuelan Carlos Network
The Italian Red Brigades
The Spanish Basque BENTA
The Spanish ETA
The West German Baader-Meinhof
The West German Red Army Faction
The Irish Republican Army

The Lebanese Minister of Information and Justice and the Attorney General announced at a press conference held for foreign reporters on 14 October 1982, that the Lebanese Armed Forces held a number of international terrorists. They uncovered a wealth of forged documents on the person of apprehended foreign nationals and in the Palestinian camps.

The find included 23,000 remarkably well forged identity cards, false passports, visas, embassy stamps, to be affixed to other forged documents, and travellers cheques.

The breakdown of international terrorists apprehended on Lebanese soil is as follows:

9 French nationals		
1 Belgian	2 British	1 West German
1 Danish national	1 Swiss	1 Dutch
1 Paraguayan	1 Swede	1 Cuban
4 Lybians	5 Iranians	1 Turk
5 Saudis	19 Egyptians	19 Iraqis
1 Qatari	4 Jordanians	6 Kuwaitis
1 Malaysian	3 Tunisians	1 Indian

The Lebanese Forces claim firm evidence that the PLO was planning a terror campaign against Jews in Europe, to be attributed to the extremist group Kataeb, a claim which sounds very plausible. The majority of the foreign terrorists in Lebanon left the country through the port of Beirut when Israel approached the city in June/July 1982. Some, dressed as Syrians, went to Damascus.

In a letter to President Reagan dated September 5, 1982, Prime Minister Begin said, "... on June 27, we suggested that all the terrorists leave Beirut and Lebanon, which they eventually did, with the help of the important good offices of Ambassador Habib, many weeks later. In the intervening battles, Israel lost 340 men killed and 2,200 wounded, 100 of them severely. Also in the battles following the rejection of our appeals by the Syrian army not to interfere, we destroyed 405 Soviet-Syrian tanks, among them nine T-72's, considered in N.A.T.O. circles to be 'invulnerable'; we downed 102 Soviet-Syrian MIG's including one MIG-25, and smashed 21 batteries of SAM-6, SAM-8 and SAM-9, a deadly weapon.

"Yet in your letter to me and in your speech to the American people, you did not, Mr. President, even mention the bravery of the Israeli fighter nor the great sacrifices of the Israeli army and people. The impression one could have gotten was that Mr. Philip Habib, with the help of the expeditionary units, achieved the result. It is my duty to tell you, Mr. President, that I was struck by the omission, I state a fact; I do not complain."

> The Lord bringeth the counsel of the heathen to nought; he maketh the devices of the people to none effect. The counsel of the Lord standeth for ever, the thoughts of his heart to all generations. Blessed is the nation whose God is the Lord; and the people whom he hath chosen for his own inheritance.[20]

---

[20] Psalm 33:10, 11, 12.

22
Operation Liberation

In June 1982 while watching the evening newscast in his comfortable Los Angeles home, Irving Boren thought out loud, "Does everyone believe these blatant lies about Israel's involvement in Lebanon?"

As a successful Jewish industrialist, he was busy and he certainly didn't need to get caught up with such current events 'on the other side of the world'. Gourmet meals at sunset in a private box at the famous Hollywood Bowl while listening to the world's greatest musicians punctuated his active life of business and pleasure. "Just forget it! Don't get involved. Leave the Middle East issues to the politicians and the media men. Relax and go to sleep!"

With such thoughts, Irving tossed and turned trying to drift off to sleep. Impossible. Finally he picked up the phone and began to search for someone to help him. Through a mutual friend, George Brokate, founder of TYJ Telemedia in Costa Mesa, California, he heard of our work in Israel. Immediately he placed a call to Jerusalem and outlined his plans to Jay for production of a TV special that would truthfully show the response of the Lebanese and Palestinian people to the widely disputed Israeli 'Operation Peace for Galilee'.

Jay recognized this as an answer to his prayer. He too had felt that in light of his work on previous productions, 'Apples of Gold' on the modern history of Israel, and 'Messiah's

Feast' on Christian Zionism, that in all fairness he should do something on the Arab Palestinian issue. This was the project.

Just a few weeks later Irving Boren, George Brokate and Don Stewart, assistant pastor to Chuck Smith at Calvary Chapel in Costa Mesa, arrived in Jerusalem eager to begin their crucial production schedule.

Final plans were quickly drawn up and contacts made with a local television crew, the Israeli Foreign Ministry, and the Israeli Defence Forces press office to obtain entry permits and military clearances. An IDF escort was assigned for security purposes.

The crew commenced on the basis of 'no preconceived ideas'. Already so much reported in the press showed Israel as the aggressor. It was decided to ask questions of the Lebanese and Palestinian people themselves and let their responses tell the real story.

Much of the media coverage given to the war in Lebanon lacked an overall dimension relating current events to the 10 year history of conflict and destruction that had brought wreck and ruin to this once beautiful country of Phoenician culture and heritage. In fact, Beirut was termed the Paris of the Middle East and the nearby mountains in winter had become of late 'Little Switzerland' with ski resorts and elegant hotels frequented by international 'jet setters'. All this had quickly changed since the arrival of the PLO following Black September 1970, and the Syrians in 1976. Beautiful Lebanon had become an international center for training terrorists and dealing death. Barbarism and anarchy had destroyed this playground and financial center of the Middle East.

The tragic indifference of western democracies was reflected in their reportage of current events in Lebanon. Not one plea for action had arisen from so-called Christian nations as daily Christian and Muslim Lebanese were being slaughtered in a horrific civil war intensified by the presence of Soviet-supplied Syrian troops and PLO gunmen. The ensuing internecine struggle across the socio-religious strata of Lebanon brought calamitous results with Lebanese loyalties being split among religious rather than national ties.

In an interview with ABC TV on July 7, 1982, Bashir Gemayel, the assassinated president-elect of Lebanon, said, "In eight years of fighting we have out of a population of three million inhabitants more than 100,000 killed, more than 300,000 wounded and almost half of the population uprooted from its homes."

Of all the countries in the world only Israel, a so-called enemy, came to the aid of Lebanon. In 1978 Israel responded to Lebanon's suffering by cutting an opening in the security fence that formed the boundary between the two countries, known as 'the good fence.' Through it came hundreds of Lebanese seeking refuge, medical aid, food, water and employment. Horror stories of the PLO antics were passed on to the Israeli authorities.

Increased PLO rocket and artillery attacks across the border brought nearly every town, hamlet and village in northern Israel under siege. Israel had no choice but to act. The PLO never once sought out military targets, but rather ambushed buses, killing and wounding school children and vacationers, stormed apartment houses and nurseries, attacked towns and villages with artillery and rocket barrages.

Israel made every effort to warn the PLO of the consequences if they kept up these attacks. Using diplomatic exchange and limited military means, Israel desperately tried to protect the lives of its citizens, many of whom slept with their families week after week in air raid shelters, but to no avail. Finally, as an act of self-defense and self-preservation, Israel launched what is known as 'Operation Peace for Galilee'. In the initial stages it was planned to create a 40 km. wide 'cordon sanitarre' clear of terrorist bases and to put Israel out of artillery range.

However, such enormous quantities of Soviet weapons

were found in Southern Lebanon, including long range artillery equipment and Katyusha rockets, that a decision was made to push the battle right to Beirut, the nerve center of PLO operations and headquarters of Yasser Arafat. Nearly without exception, Israel's action met with disapproval in the world press. Instead of liberator, she was labelled an aggressor and invader.

As the video crew made its way into Lebanon through the scenic Rosh Hanikra checkpoint on the Mediterranean coast, a change was immediately evident. The rocky, mountainous topography contrasted with the lush coastal plain of northern Israel. Lebanese fishermen, prohibited from using their boats and nets during the heavy battles of the previous weeks, now eagerly began to ply their trade. Signs of warfare were clearly noticeable but not nearly as widespread as indicated by the press. Houses and commercial locations had been damaged without any consistency. We later found out that the IDF forces had moved house by house through this area cleansing it of PLO terrorists. Only where they drew gunfire did they retaliate. The PLO had carefully chosen civilian locations to provide their cover.

Jay reports: "Certainly damage had occurred but it was not as widespread as we anticipated. Everywhere the industrious indomitable Lebanese were busy rebuilding. In the aftermath of a war that had lasted eight years, their courage and grit was inspiring. We made our way to Rashidiyah, one of the famous Palestinian refugee camps of Lebanon just south of Tyre. We were not prepared for the frank statements and horror stories we were about to encounter. As we turned west off the main north-south highway into the camp, we were immediately shocked by the contrasting sights. Israeli bulldozers had cleared a roadway through the rubble at the entrance to the camp. It was obvious that an armed struggle had occurred. However, the local population were not in the least intimidated by the presence of the Israeli Army. We were later to understand why."

As we stopped our minibus in the heart of the camp, children and curious onlookers immediately surrounded us. Here was our chance to speak to *real* Palestinian refugees. The one burning question was now about to be answered.

'As you have been stateless for 34 years since leaving Palestine, are you now dreaming of returning to a Palestinian state on the West Bank?' The answers were transcribed exactly word for word but the names have been shortened to protect them from PLO reprisals.

ABDEL: "I am willing, all the people in this camp are willing, to stay here. We heard that the PLO want to take us to the Bekaa Valley. Even if they build us a palace, we refuse to move from here. It has been our home for 34 years. My son is in Lybia, my daughter studies medicine in Russia."

SULIMAN: "We lived and worked here since 1948, sent our children first to UNRWA schools and then abroad to America for higher education as engineers and architects. I have a son in Havana studying telecommunications and another son in Kuwait. Even if driven out by force, we refuse to move from here."

UNIDENTIFIED WOMAN: "We ask for our husbands and children, they did not fight the Israeli Defence Forces. Those who fought moved to West Beirut. Here there was no resistance, we surrendered as we were asked to do. We believe Israel is a very fine country, one of the best. We were all born here, and we don't want to go anywhere else. I send regards to my mother in Saudi Arabia, my brother in East Germany.

"Bring back our young men who were taken prisoners, these young men belong to those who came here in 1948. They have no guilt, and they were taken by force by the PLO who came here from Jordan after King Hussein threw them out of his country. They compelled us by force, they were stronger than us and the Lebanese army. They went to the schools and enrolled teenagers by force. We ask for compassion and mercy for these kids.

"Tracts were distributed by the Israelis asking us during the war to wave white flags and surrender, so we did. We want peace. We are cousins to the Israelis and would like to live in peace, and we have the best esteem and profound respect for Israel."

IBN SAID: "On behalf of the people here, I want to thank you for giving us a chance to speak to the world. We here in Kefr Senin fully support the PLO claims which are just and human and minimal. We want peace and we want a Palestinian state. There are other Palestinians who would like to stay in Lebanon if the government agrees."

AN UNIDENTIFIED MAN told the film crew, "My 12 year old was kidnapped, taken out of school and recruited by the PLO to be a killer in U.N. supported schools. Boys learned to run the rocket launchers. Schools of terror were held in basements, large caches of ammunition were stored there as well. Rented houses were transferred into military bases. You couldn't complain or you'd lose your neck. We are surrounded by a sea of hostility."

ABDUL: "I'm 63 and have been living here since 1943. I've now spent as many years in Palestine as I've spent here."

MUHAMED: "I'd like to stay here in Rashidiyah, as do all the others both young and old, we've been here since 1948."

HILME: "All that we urgently request is that we be left here in Rashidiyah camp. Our reasons are first, we've been here for 34 years and we have become acclimatized. We have our work here and our children were born here, which means we have become used to this place."

AN UNIDENTIFIED WOMAN standing with a child in her arms: "We do not wish for Palestine back. I and my husband and my children were born here in Lebanon, we do not accept any other place."

As we began to conclude this set of interviews a car drove up and the Palestinian driver, obviously a member of the refugee camp, began to speak to us in rapid Hebrew. We were curious as to how he obtained his knowledge of the language and found out that just prior to 1948 he had married a Jewish woman from Haifa whose mother tongue was Hebrew. She had spent the past 34 years in a Palestinian refugee camp at her husband's side.

A REFUGEE: In the shadow of Beaufort Castle, an old man was trying to put a little house together. He had this to say: "I am Diab Moussa, a Palestinian. I left the village of Honen on the border of Lebanon and Israel in the year 1942 and came here to Lebanon. Concerning the future I prefer to live in Lebanon. My sons are here, and I wish I could be a naturalized Lebanese, a citizen with full rights and live here."

THE LEBANESE

Everywhere we went we received candid answers to questions such as, "Tell us about your experience in Lebanon these last few years." Here are a few random quotes we received from the Lebanese, including Muslims, Christian Phalangists, and refugees.

HAMED HEMEDAH, Lebanese: "I am a student in the Lebanese University second year faculty of law. We had to stop studies in our second year because of the PLO bombs. We have the feeling that nobody cares about us. We suffered too much these last eight years, and cannot support it any more. We wish the Lebanese army could get the control all over Lebanon."

UNIDENTIFIED YOUNG LEBANESE, Maronite Christian: "I am a Lebanese from the south, we thank the state of Israel who delivered us from the destroyers, the Muharabeen, the PLO. They burned our religion, slaughtered us, took our goods and income. We hope to be delivered from all foreigners, in a free independent Lebanon, no east and no west."

A CHRISTIAN PHALANGIST: "The PLO are not human beings at all. They are ready to kill even a baby because he is a Christian. They should not be sent anywhere, or given any choice, they should be buried dead deep under the ground."

Feelings ran very deep, throwing light on the hatred behind the Sabra and Shatilla massacres which shocked the world only weeks later.

2nd PHALANGIST: "The Palestinians kidnapped me, I suffered a lot in the Sabra camp, I was disfigured and burned. I was kidnapped because I am a Christian. After suffering one whole month, I succeeded in running away. It was four years ago that I escaped from PLO controlled West Beirut and moved to live in East Beirut."

3rd PHALANGIST: "Three months ago I was arrested in West Beirut, after they burned our home. The PLO are not human beings, no civilized person can live with them. They should be sent to Syria because the Syrians are sewage like them; they all should be taken to the desert and burned."

Over and over again, through such statements, it was clearly shown that the innocent Palestinians and Lebanese had become victims of Lebanese power politics and PLO propaganda. In Lebanon a delicate balance exists between the Muslims and the Christians. The majority rules the nation. Hence the refugees, mainly Muslim, were never given rights to citizenship lest they upset the ratio. Thus the politicians began to search for ways and means of expressing self-determination. The PLO then used this phrase 'Palestinian rights' to justify the establishment of itself as a terror organization.

In casual conversation we gradually detected from some of the refugees an attitude of smouldering hostility toward the PLO. The extravagant lifestyle of the PLO leadership naturally evoked feelings of bitterness and resentment among the Palestinians still forced to live in the camps. These people were readily used by the PLO to convey an image of poverty to the world, but a 'poverty' manipulated by what is probably the wealthiest terrorist organization in history.

Abass al-Haj, 55, a longtime resident of the Ein Hilwe refugee camp, said in an interview in the independent Ha'aretz daily: "The condition of the inhabitants of the camp was very bad, but the commanders of the PLO did wonderfully well for themselves. They drove expensive cars, some of which were stolen. For years the Arab states gave millions for us, the Palestinians, but there was never money to build a sewage system for our camp."[1]

We then headed north toward Tyre and were constantly aware by visual evidence of how the PLO had strategically located weapons and ammunition in densely populated civilian areas in the hope that this would either deter Israeli attacks or exact a price from Israel in world opinion for killing civilians. Towns and camps were turned into vast underground shelters and anti-aircraft guns were placed in schoolyards, among apartment houses, next to churches and hospitals. The remains of the shelters could be readily seen soon after the fighting, and the local Palestinians and Lebanese can still point out the sites.

It seems this strategy of hiding behind civilians was entirely natural for the terrorist organization whose greatest exploits in the past invariably involved hijacking, and the killing of innocent bystanders.

Our next stop was in the home of a medical doctor in Tyre. The tension and pressure of the last eight years had etched its way into lines of fatigue, sorrow, and heartache on his face. He spoke carefully but candidly.

DOCTOR: "Lebanon was raped by the PLO, raped! Rape in the United States is a very horrible crime. Physically and mentally and morally, Lebanon was raped. They were taking everything and they gave nothing. They were killing children, women, old men, young men, just sometimes for known reasons and other times for unknown reasons.

"What they did in Lebanon showed clearly that they are bandits, outlaws, creeps, they didn't use any principles nor moral values, no sign of civilization. They didn't respect anybody. They hired the lowest outlaws, nameless people.

"They claim to have a cause. A cause. A definite target with

[1] Ha'aretz Daily, August 20, 1982.

definite aims, and means to achieve these aims. The PLO did nothing to achieve these aims. Their claims to go back to Palestine and the right to establish their state. That is the question, this is not my business but theirs.

"From my experience there is only one way to treat the PLO. Either you tyrannize them or they terrorize you. It means that Prime Minister Begin was left with only one way to deal with them, strongly and with force. In this way in my modest opinion, Begin is not an extremist nor a racist, but a realistic man walking on the right way. He had no other choice, he couldn't afford to make a mistake. If he did, he and his people would be destroyed too. So he did it, fortunately for him and for us."

IRVING: "How do you view the Israeli action of entering Lebanon during Operation Peace for Galilee?"

DOCTOR: Drawing a deep breath, "It was freedom for us, they did the same job that the Allies did in freeing Europe in 1945."

IRVING: "What is your attitude now toward the Israeli Defence Forces?"

DOCTOR: "I love them. I will tell my children also to love them forever because of one thing, they have saved our lives, that's enough. They saved our dignity, our lives, our independence, our existence. In two terms I want to tell you, God gave us life; Israel gave us liberty and dignity. I hope that our two countries will be tied together in the future with bonds of mutual respect and friendship."

IRVING: "Doctor, what you have told us is very touching. Are you frightened for your family in the future since you have been so candid with us?"

DOCTOR: "I know that the truth has a price and sometimes a ransom. The truth that I have told you may cost me my life. I am very aware of this fact. The loss of my life would be a very modest contribution to express gratitude to Israel and the Jewish people, and a modest contribution on behalf of the Lebanese. A free Lebanese voice has told the Arab people as well as the world the very truth of the matter."

As the sun set we drove back hurriedly to Israel, since the IDF would not, at that time, give permission for civilians to stay overnight in Lebanon. Upon arriving back in Israel, Jay was overwhelmed by a sense of new-found pride in the Jewish nation he had chosen to call home. Everywhere the sound of sprinklers and the smell of blossoms spoke to him of the order and prosperity of this tiny nation. Arabs and Jews *could* live together in peace and harmony. The lights of Arab villages and Israeli kibbutzim and moshavim glistened in the moonlight in close proximity to one another, very proof of this fact. He was proud to be an Israeli by adoption.

BEIRUT

The following morning we decided to go straight to Beirut. On the way we passed through the areas we had visited the previous day and then went on to Sidon, Damour and by noon to Beirut. From the IDF press headquarters on a hill about two miles from the downtown area, East Beirut lay sprawled out in front of us with West Beirut in the background. Amidst sporadic machine gun fire and artillery barrages, we panned the TV cameras from the rooftop of a nearby apartment block. The friendly Lebanese inhabitants asked us to please work quickly as they didn't want our presence to draw artillery fire from nearby PLO gun encampments. We agreed and left rapidly.

We were then given a Lebanese escort furnished by the IDF military spokesman. He directed us down back streets and through deserted alleys until finally we were at Gallerie Simaan, the traffic circle that marked the boundary area between Lebanese controlled East Beirut and the PLO controlled West Beirut. The roads were jammed with traffic. Many cars and trucks were crammed with people and personal effects as thousands of Lebanese were escaping from West Beirut. Others were returning from the north to their deserted homes in the south now that the threat of the PLO terrorists had been removed. Our 'guide' led us in our vehicle closer and closer to downtown East Beirut until finally we spotted the famous harbor front dotted with exclusive hotels that now lay in smoking ruins.

We were on our way to the home of May Murr, a very well known author, historian and lecturer in Beirut. We travelled through rubble strewn streets with Israeli tanks and Lebanese troops stationed behind piles of sandbags at various intervals. We finally arrived at the apartment block surrounded by high buildings in the downtown area. We clamoured into the elevator with all our equipment and we realized that we had arrived at the home of a cultured family. The interview in the living room was completed in the adjacent dining room. A delicious French lunch, served on a linen tablecloth with fine silverware, was hosted by the affable Mrs. Murr, a renowned Lebanese lady of letters. She spoke forcibly and with emotion.

"We have had eight years of war and the world didn't know anything about this war, nothing about the atrocities and the horrors. Everything in Lebanon is destroyed, all the houses crushed . . . If you go to our museum now, you will see that there is nothing left. I cried yesterday. I cried. I am one of the historians of Lebanon and I cried. The destruction is everywhere. You can only believe if you go and see yourself. Our museum is totally demolished. We had artifacts from the very beginning of all civilization."

Later that day, Hareth Boustany the former director of the National Muesum in Beirut, said, "I was shocked to see what they did in this building. And all of these things were of our culture, of Caananite and Phoenician culture, some 6,000 years of history. In the Geneva Convention it states that no army is allowed to enter any museum because in these places there is the storehouse of all the cultural history of a people. They took no notice."

Mr. Boren asked Mrs. Murr, "What is your experience here in Beirut with the PLO?"

MRS. MURR: "In Israel now there are arms for more than one half million people. Arms found by Israel in Lebanon over the last few weeks. Our army has 24 tanks, and the PLO has 400 or 500 tanks. I don't know any other country that has had a war for eight years and has resisted as we resisted without arms, and without billions of petro-dollars. These were arms for terrorist activity.

"Beirut is now the center of all the terrorist operations in the world. The man who killed Aldo Moro in Italy went to Rome from Beirut. And the man who tried to kill King Faisal also went from Beirut. Agca, who tried to kill the Pope went from Beirut. All the international terrorists were trained here.

"We said to the world, 'You are not courageous. You are terrorized by Arafat. You haven't got the courage to tell the truth. You, Mitterrand, you, President Reagan, haven't the courage to say the truth. We expect more from you than you gave because in the West and especially in America, you have to safeguard this land of truth. Lebanon is a land of truth and civilization. You can't just give it to the terrorists of the world.'

"They were our worst enemy. The greatest enemy from all of our history, and I am an historian and I say, this is the PLO. You see, Ibn Haldon said in every country where Arabism has gone it has destroyed that country. The great historian of the Arab people said this. This word is true."

QUESTION: "What about the young people in Lebanon who are confronted with this enormous problem of divided loyalties?"

MRS. MURR: "I spoke to my students in the military college three days after the Operation Peace for Galilee.

"The students asked me, 'What do you think about the military invasion by our enemy Israel?'

"'The invasion?' I said, 'Call it an operation for salvation.'"

We also spoke to a respected Muslim lawyer in Beirut, Dr.

Muhamed Mograbi, and his comments were particularly meaningful as his home had just been destroyed in West Beirut.

QUESTION: "What is your opinion of what has been occurring here in Lebanon in these last few weeks?"

DR. MOGRABI: "Lebanon is a victim. A victim of foreign pressure, foreign intervention and foreign feuds. We have had many participants in this ugly story over the past years. The Palestinians are the main actors in this tragedy, also the Syrians, and all of the Arab countries, and of course Israel.

"As a result of all of these efforts by our neighbors and world powers, including the United States of America, Lebanon has been systematically destroyed and devastated over the past years. The Palestinians have been permitted to build up their forces in Lebanon and establish a strong base in West Beirut and in Southern Lebanon. I wish that the Palestinians never came to Lebanon, and that we never had the PLO in Beirut. I wish that the Lebanese government had been strong enough to resist all these foreign pressures and to prevent these foreigners from forcing on us the state of affairs that led to this destruction. We have to blame the great powers. The United States looked favorably on the establishment and the build-up of PLO power in Lebanon. The Palestinians came into Lebanon as refugees and were so well treated that they liked the house and decided to take it over. Our government is not only facing a problem of military intervention, it's a question of power politics. Outside powers are financing, promoting and sponsoring local groups and factions, parasites who are able to grow and play a significant role with the foreign support, finances and sponsorship. We have to blame many of the Arab powers that have spent money and financed the export of ammunition, mercenaries, and equipment into Lebanon and thereby financed the terror and devastation."

QUESTION: "What about the Israeli involvement in Lebanon?"

DR. MOGRABI: "The Israeli Army came to Lebanon

without the prior permission or consent of the Lebanese and I resent the Israeli presence in Lebanon as much as I resent every other foreign presence. But I would not focus on Israel, I would not place the blame on Israel. Certainly, Israel is partly to blame, but it is not number one on the list. I think that number one on the list is our neighbor, the Syrians. They came before the Israelis and we thought that they came as peacemakers, but they actually became another army of occupation. Unfortunately, the Israeli Operation Peace for Galilee has taken too long, particularly against Beirut. If the Israelis had finished their job in the first week of the invasion then certainly we would have had only about 10% of the damage and destruction that we have suffered in Beirut. Our home in West Beirut has been hit at least a half a dozen times over the last six weeks, and if this military operation had been finalized in the first week, then our home maybe would have been saved along with hundreds of others.

"I don't understand the moral justification for the Palestinian resistance in Beirut. I don't understand the moral justification for the pressures by the world powers against Israel to limit their actions. They certainly must know that the PLO have brought this calamity upon Beirut, but I also do not understand the moral justification for the Israeli attack, for the role of policeman outside his own jurisdiction. I wish this thing had been organized somehow between the Israelis and the Lebanese government, even in secret. What about tomorrow? I would like to see the Palestinians out, the PLO out, the Syrians out, and the Israelis out."

By September 1982, with the election of Bashir Gemayel as the president of Lebanon, it was hoped that this young charismatic leader could unite all the factions in Lebanon to build a new order in the war-torn little nation. Their hopes were shattered when only one week before he was to take office, in a move that sent shock waves around the world, he was assassinated by a huge bomb.

A new PLO extemist group claimed responsibility for the

bombing. This set the stage for the subsequent revenge massacres by Gemayel's Phalangists in the Sabra and Shatilla Palestinian refugee camps.

Before his death, Bashir Gemayel said in a film interview: "We are surrounded by a sea of hostility. We were left alone in this part of the world and what the Arab world and the entire world doesn't understand is that we were fighting for our independence and for our sovereignty. Even if Lebanon is very small, it will be easy to eat, but impossible to digest. This is what we are suffering from now. The Syrians slew innocent civilians with a conscious, deliberate action. The holocaust is continuing day in and day out. They have entered Lebanon to accomplish a whole program of murder and this with the blessing of the super powers.

"We have always believed in our destiny, in our destiny of free people. Our children are growing up under the strains of warfare imposed upon us under a permanent threat of immolation."[2]

PLO DETAINEE CAMPS

With these words ringing in our ears, we made our way southward along the coastal road toward the Ansara PLO detainee camp. The previous day we had made arrangements with the Israeli commanding officer of the area to allow us to enter the camp and to speak directly to some PLO terrorists. We were eager to keep our appointment at 3:00 p.m. However, the traffic buildup on the road between Damour and Sidon and between Sidon and Tyre proved to be so congested that we arrived at Ansara at 5:15 p.m. It was decided after a briefing session by the camp commander that it was more practical to do the interviews the following day. Of course we were disappointed but Jay knew the Lord had brought the crew there for a specific purpose. Climbing up the bulldozed

---

[2] Bashir Gemayel, in film called Resistance and Aggression, produced by Lebanese Forces Command, Department of Information, October 1979.

embankments behind which the 9,000 PLO detainees were held, Jay looked out over the massive concentration of murderers and began to realize that they were men just like any other human beings, and they needed most of all not his condemnation, but his prayers.

The following day we arrived in good time for our interviews and were ushered into a parking area alongside the detainee camp. We quickly set up our equipment and turned an IDF tent, normally used as a dining area, into a television studio. When we were ready, we gave the signal to the commander and he in turn ordered the entrance of the terrorists one by one. Our first impression of these men was how young they were, and secondly, that they were not intimidated by the IDF guards.In fact, many of them joked together in Arabic, as Israelis growing up in Israel often learn to speak Arabic almost as well as their native Hebrew.

The first terrorist came forward, shook hands with us and sat down behind the microphone. Carefully we introduced the purpose of our interview.

QUESTION: "What can you tell us about the events that have occurred in Lebanon in the last few years?"

PLO TERRORIST: "The malicious people who promoted the Lebanese-Palestinian war, or the internal Lebanese war, have become accustomed to killing. If they met someone they did not like, they would simply pull out their gun and kill him. Who would question them? They are thieves and robbers. These are the things that we could not and do not speak about."

QUESTION: "What was your part in the recent events in this area?"

PLO TERRORIST: "I was a member of the organization, and I confess it regretfully. I was compelled and mobilized to enroll in the PLO without any serious training. There were no decent commanders. The officers needed bodyguards so as not to be killed by members of other organizations in the PLO. Throughout the years we lived here in Lebanon the atmosphere was one of mobilization against the Israeli people and against America. I'm speaking frankly and not just because I'm speaking to the American television. The Arab countries mobilized us against Israel as the 'Zionist state' that exterminates the Arabs.

"Then they created for us what is called the Palestinian Revolution, and this Palestinian Revolution was not built on one organization but upon a multitude of endless organizations and groups. Each time there was a crisis or a feud between Hassad and Arafat, or between Hussein and Arafat, we fought and the result was the killing of thousands of Palestinians. This fighting between all the different factions is how we became known as the 'muharabeen' or the destructors. Since we stopped fighting Israel we have started fighting each other. Arab leaders were very critical of the peace that was concluded with Israel through the Camp David agreements. In the Arab world, Egypt was called reactionary, capitalist and opportunist. The Arab states, and Saudi Arabia especially, proclaimed a 'jihad' or holy war for us. But while they are talking, we are killing each other and robbing and slaughtering our own people.

"The leaders are rotten. Syria and our 'ally' the Soviet Union, together with all the socialist regimes and states fed us lies. We were told America is our enemy, and what happened then? There was not positive results from the Soviet people or from the Syrians or the Jordanians or any of the others, who bought terrorist groups with money in order to fight. Syria continually attacks America but the Americans did no harm to them.

"Why are the Syrians in Lebanon anyway, what are their intentions? Are they planning to stay on? Everyone knew that Israel did not destroy and did not kill wantonly. The Syrians caused the destruction and killing here and so did we, the PLO.

"Israel is stronger not because of the arms they have, but because they are united and help each other. We fight one another. Our leaders robbed the financial aid sent to help our poor people. Haj Ishmael, the well-known commander of the PLO in Sidon, forced the university to deliver him a B.A. certificate at their graduation ceremonies by threatening them with his guns. Everyone knows that is the way they rule Lebanon.

"Don't listen to Arafat or Hassad, they speak nonsense. They are cheating. They are used to killing and lying, it's their way of life. We want a new life. We want the U.S. and Israel to help us to have peace. We want to live in Lebanon under Lebanese law. We want justice.

"Here in the camp we feel as equal human beings with the Israeli officers. It was not like that with the Arab officers, they were hard and cruel on us, and to one another. I am the Mukhtar, head commander in this camp of about 400 PLO prisoners. We are free now to rule our own life. We have become human beings. We insist on the fact that we are fed up with the hatred and the violence, with the use of the rotten guns and arms. The Israeli military police treat us well. Believe me, despite the fact that I have children outside in this very vicinity, it is safer for me to stay here and not leave until there is peace outside the camp.

"I beg the Arab peoples in this area not to believe the leaders preaching Socialism and Communism and attacking the U.S. Not a single peace initiative was undertaken by any of these countries, they don't want peace and freedom. They like killing. All the initiatives for peace were backed by the U.S., who want freedom and peace. There are thousands of Palestinians able to study in the U.S. and pray as Muslims but in Russia while they are there the authorities are fighting against religion and against personal freedoms. In Israel, there is harmony and co-existence between the three religions, the Christians, Jews and Muslims. We don't want to be Communist poor, we prefer to live well and free.

"The Lebanese wound is very deep. The PLO destroyed Lebanon. They brought in mercenaries from foreign countries. They were careless with the lives of the local Palestinians and the Lebanese people. They brought complete anarchy to Lebanon. Please, I want to live in peace with Israel. If I said this before, I would be put in jail by the PLO as a traitor, but now I am free to say that we want humanity and democracy, and I say this all as a free man, free of any pressure. The Israeli government asked us to surrender and we actually did and none of us died. It is true that we are detained and prisoners, but we are alive. We can live longer and we can return to our countries, but he who is still carrying a gun has never brought a solution.

"We lived ten years in bitterness and sadness, ten years which were the spring of our lives. Since I was 16 I have not been aware of anything but bullets. What kind of a life is this? Should we also teach our children and make them aware only of bullets? No, by God, we do not agree. We have lived in Lebanon for all our lives and we want to eventually go back to live under the Lebanese authorities according to whatever laws they legislate."

2nd PLO TERRORIST, Achmed, born in Sidon, Lebanon: "I enrolled to serve for the PLO militia of the Saika Division from 1973 to 1976. Saika is a PLO sub-group under Syrian control. In 1976 Fatah, the biggest terrorist group in the PLO headed by Arafat, arrested us and accused us of treason and betrayal.[3] I was put in jail. In 1977 there was a compulsory mobilization and we were freed from jail and mobilized or else we would have been left there languishing or killed by the PLO.

"Here in this Israeli camp I never dreamed Israel would treat us like this, their behavior is fine. I have attended two different sessions of investigations, without any violence or use of force. Imagine, questions without being hit. If you asked me to go back to Acre in Palestine, I refuse. I have built

[3] Note: 1976 was the year of the disagreement between the Syrian army and the PLO in Lebanon.

a life here for 30 years in Sidon, and don't want to start all over again. Besides, no Arab country will give us a passport, we are stateless, no one wants us, we have found the Arabs all are liars."

3rd PLO TERRORIST, Ibrahim: "The Jews and Palestinians are cousins and that means we should always live together for we belong to the same family. Unfortunately, our Arab leaders tried to 'embrace' us by putting us in refugee camps and giving us the lowest kind of life. We have no rights of our own, we are left in slums as dirty people. I opened a bakery in the refugee camp El-Buss in 1974. The Israelis attacked the headquarters of the terrorist organization called 'The General Command' which was close to the bakery, so it was also destroyed. I accepted a proposition to work as a guard in the terrorist organization, and part time as a baker. Then I started working in the administration and finance department of the organization called the 'Front of Arab Liberation', a PLO sub-group. In January 1982 I stopped working for this organization and opened a bake shop in my house. I've done well.

"The organizations of the PLO were not able to co-exist with the Jewish state. Israel claims the right to be recognized and to live in peace, but the PLO insist on having the whole of Palestine and they work continuously to get Israel out of the region. This is unrealistic. The Jewish people lived in the land for many thousands of years before us and have the right to exist as we do.

"We have tried to live in other Arab countries but their behavior is very bad, no culture, no decent jobs, no education, and no freedom makes it a very unhappy life. I prefer to go to Australia, Germany, or the USA, or any other country, but not to an Arab country. The Arab countries do not give the Palestinians any basic rights at all, we are victims of the Arab leaders."

4th PLO TERRORIST, Tawil: "We were told to leave Haifa in 1948 by the Arab nations. They said it was for just a couple of days, with a firm promise that we would be back very soon. We were taken to Syria, then to Aleppo on the coast, where we were very badly treated and considered traitors. I escaped and came back to Lebanon. I have lived very nicely in Sidon for the last 35 years. When the destroyers, the PLO, started making troubles, I escaped with my family to Jordan. I worked all this last year in Jordan in order to put my children in Jordanian schools. But before I could do so I had to have a certificate from Lebanon, and so I am here to get it. Then the Israeli military actions began.

"We are all well treated by the IDF and we thank God that they delivered us from the PLO. Since they came in no one has hurt or humiliated me. I wish to live in Jordan because my family is there." Tawil is crying by this time. "We want peace for our children. God has helped us to be delivered from all these rotten Arab countries. The 'muharabeen' have destroyed our homes, stolen our children, and beat us. They beat me, and imprisoned me in a toilet. Look at me, I'm an old man, 55 years old. We want peace with the help of God.

"I used to live in Haifa. I lived there with the Israeli people. My neighbor was a Rabbi. I believe that peace will come. The victory will be for Israel because Israel is human and Israelis love each other and work hard for the benefit of the whole country. All Arabs are liars. Already we are living with the Lebanese people for 34 years in the spirit and love of Jesus . . . I ask all loving people in the world to go hand in hand with Begin and raise their hand in a march of peace. We were deeply touched by the death of Sadat, because he raised the flag of peace. May his soul rest in peace."

5th PLO TERRRIST, Salem: "The Arab nations did not give us a chance to live. They fed us on a dream of a homeland while they squandered their income on entertainment in France and U.S.A. They sent us some money, but they have refused to naturalize us in their respective countries or accept us among them. Nations like Canada and Australia and others give their nationality to Palestinians after five years of living there. Here for example, in Lebanon, after 34 years we are still refused Lebanese citizenship, despite the fact that I was born here and have lived here for 22 years.

"The Arab nations raised us on a dream that hurt us. They pretended to deal with our cause in the United Nations, but they betrayed us by refusing to give the Palestinians either a chance to be assimilated or a possibility to live in peace. The Arab countries and Muslims watched us die without raising a hand. They want to keep us living as slaves. Anywhere in the Arab world they see us as low grade people, fit only for death. This is why as many as possible of our young people run away."

AN OLD MAN: "When they took my son, I knew he was in safe hands. We thank the IDF and Major Haddad who fathered us. I know and I am ready to tell it to anybody that disaster has come from the Arab states."

As the interviews drew to a close we were truly deeply moved by what we had heard and by the candid explanations of these so-called terrorists. We realized that for the first time perhaps in their lives they were able to express themselves freely without fear of death or reprisals. As we left the camp we were aware that there was only one way for the detainees to go and that was the road of peace. Without that objective their lives would remain in the chaotic confusion of the past eight years.

LIFE IN THE DETENTION CAMP

The camp had provided a certain amount of order. The detainees arise at 5:30 each morning and are provided with three meals a day, which they cook. At breakfast they receive their daily food allotment, which is sufficient for three full meals. This includes fresh vegetables, beans, meat, eggs, fresh fruit, tea, one loaf of bread per man per day, salt, sugar, yellow cheese, oil, jam, rice, and tomato sauce. Each detainee receives 5 cigarettes per day. The living conditions of detainees and their IDF guards are almost identical. Both are provided with similar food, with minor modifications, drinking water, and blankets. Though the detainees had in the past been accustomed to drinking water drawn from the local sources, they are now given potable water transported by the IDF tankers. Both detainees and IDF guards are housed in tents, while special accommodations were being erected for each group for the winter season. The detainees are issued two sets of blue or brown uniforms and are provided with underwear, soap, toothbrushes, toothpaste, razor blades, etc. They were also provided with cleaning materials for the daily housekeeping chores. In each cell block they were permitted to launder their own clothes and cook their own food on stoves supplied by camp authorities. Religious services are held daily. The Mukhtar is in contact regularly with the camp commander to solve whatever problems may arise. It was strictly forbidden to strike detainees or to carry a baton of any sort. This prohibition also extends to the detainees themselves.

At the time of our interview the future of the detainees was being decided. By the end of 1982, of the 9,064 persons arrested, 3,147 had already been released. The government of Israel had informed the Red Cross that as of October 4, 1982, she was willing to release 700 non-Lebanese or Palestinians, but by November only 200 of these were freed, among them two Frenchmen, one Austrian, two Norwegians and one Canadian, due to the time taken over the Red Cross procedures. It should be noted that in many cases the Red Cross requested that a number of detainees slated for release not be freed because their safety could not be guaranteed after their release.

During this time many television crews, investigating committees and reporters came to Lebanon to examine the facts. One of these was a group that included Congressman Charles Wilson from the United States, and following his visit he said on Israel television, "In our times of questioning in Lebanon I would keep the Israelis a long way from where I was questioning so they couldn't be seen. I'd walk down small alley ways and find someone who spoke English and then ask them questions. In that context others would join them and add in their comments. We got a total unanimity of the pleasure and relief that the Israeli army had freed them from the PLO and the Syrians. I certainly was surprised at the Arabs that we spoke to in Nabatiya, of the various stories they told of atrocities and mistreatment under the PLO."

ATROCITIES

One such story was relayed by the mukhtar of the Muslim village of Burj Bahal, who told of a horrifying incident that occurred in 1981 in Sidon. A man had been sentenced to death by a Fatah military court for 'collaboration' with Israel. The reason: a pair of shoes made in Israel had been found in his possession. He was then taken to the center of the square, his feet and wrists chained to the bumpers of four separate cars, a pistol was fired as a signal, and the cars drove off in different directions. This dreadful execution has been confirmed by numerous witnesses. The catalogue of PLO crimes against the Lebanese, both Christians and Muslims, is long and monstrous. In addition there was continual theft, blackmail, extortion, arson, kidnapping, rape and bullying.[4]

Newspapers around the world carried the picture of the body of an Israeli helicopter pilot stuffed into the trunk of a car and paraded through the streets of Sidon with his feet dragging in the street. A teenager shot the helicopter down on June 6, 1982, with a katyusha rocket launcher.The extent of barbarism and sadistic depth is expressed by a social worker in southern Lebanon who said, "You see kids who tie rats behind their bicycles because they have seen grown-ups tie prisoners up behind their jeeps."

Dr. Hassan Hamoud, the owner-director of the largest and best-equipped hospital in Sidon, said, "It was when the PLO

[4] Los Angeles Herald Examiner, July 13, 1982.

broke into the operating theater and forced us to stop surgery and to treat their wounded instead of the patient in question,and badly beat one of the doctors who refused to obey them, that I realized they were beasts from the jungle."[5]

Hamoud, who earned his medical degree from the University of Bonn in West Germany, is a Sunni Moslem who shares the resentment of Lebanon's Christians of the PLO. "They posed as national heroes fighting the Zionist enemy. In fact, over 90% of the PLO patients treated by us were wounded in clashes and quarrels among themselves.

"Many parents of rape victims brought their daughters to this hospital for treatment, where many of the young girls were found to be pregnant. An illegal 'abortion industry' developed in the camps, where girls often died under the primitive surgery conditions.

"They call it a revolution, if so, it is the dirtiest and most wicked, the richest and most brutal one in history. Every junior officer in the PLO used to race through our streets in a brand new Mercedes with machine guns sticking out.

"Their conduct inside the hospital was equally intolerable. Every time a PLO patient needed a nurse, he would simply fire his pistol at the ceiling."[6]

Ali Bader Al-Din, the imam, or Muslim pastor, of Arouf in southern Lebanon, refused to inject Palestinian nationalist themes into his sermons at his village mosque. A few days later his body was found by a shepherd under a bridge in a nearby field.

The Christian school north of Nabatiya was run by seven nuns before the PLO took over. One of the sisters told this story: "At first they kidnapped Sister C. and raped her. Then they beat the rest of us. We hid in the cellars of the monastery for 18 months. Food was brought to us at night by the local

---

[5] Ma'ariv Daily, July 16, 1982.

[6] Ibid.

Christians. For seven years the bells of our monastery did not ring."[7]

"When the PLO searched the home of a factory worker in Jezzine, they found only the man's 70 year old grandmother. They threatened her until she revealed the family's valuables which they robbed, then they raped and killed her."[8]

"A notorious rape concerns the mukhtar of Ansar, whose political statements made him unpopular with the PLO. One night they attacked his village and surrounded his house. They tied up the mukhtar and his wife, and forced them to watch as they raped their daughter, killed her, sliced off her breasts and left her mutilated body on their doorstep. This incident was also witnesed by a number of the villagers."[9]

An old prison in the casbah quarter of Sidon served as a torture center for the PLO's political opponents. One room was set aside for rape. Hassan Abed Al-Hamid related the following incident to an Israel Radio reporter: "The prison was built in 1973 and many families were locked up there. At night they would bring young girls to the office. In a special room used for the purpose, the girls could be heard screaming. After a while there was only silence. A photo of Arafat was found over the bed where the atrocities were committed. Sidon's residents said they could hear the screams of the girls almost nightly from nearby streets."[10]

Although the Israeli operation was triggered by a massive, 24-hour PLO-born bombardment of 23 Galilean towns and villages, it was undertaken as a response to 17 years of PLO terror which had claimed over 7,500 civilian casualties.[11]

---

[7] AT Magazine, August 1982.

[8] Ibid.

[9] Jerusalem Post, July 23, 1982.

[10] Israel Television, July 13, 1982.

[11] "The PLO" Department of Information, World Zionist Organization, P.O. Box 92, Jerusalem.

MOTIVATION BY HATRED

As Westerners we find it almost totally incomprehensible to empathize with the strong religious, nationalistic and cultural emotions that inflame passions to acts of violence in the Middle East. Truly we are outsiders looking in. In June 1982 during the Lebanese war, we were interceding on behalf of Israel and the Lord gave me a vision in which I was reminded of the death of Saul and his sons on Mount Gilboa. The Bible story was re-enacted before my eyes. I was shocked and said nothing about it. The account is found in I Samuel Chapter 31, verses 8 to 13. I saw how their bodies were mutilated with great delight by the attacking army, later nailed to a wall in Beth Shan, a nearby town in biblical Israel.

Less than 24 hours later, we met a young man over dinner. We had not previously met this man, and no sooner had we sat down to eat than he began to relate an experience he had witnessed just a couple of days previously while on duty in Damascus.

He began by saying, "I don't understand why I'm going to tell you this but I just feel that I have to." He began his story moved by emotion. He said, "Two wounded Israeli soldiers were brought into the ambulance entrance of a large Damascus hospital. Before the men could be carried any further into the hospital, the staff descended upon them with loud, angry and crazed shouts of triumph. Their Israeli uniforms were stripped from their broken bodies and immediately burned with great ceremony over a hastily made fire in the courtyard. Women from the vicinity began to shout and warble in the Arabic fashion with great emotion. Next the Israelis were used as human dart boards as knives were flung from many quarters of the angry crowd of locals which joined in the activity by this time. The Israelis were castrated and their right hands cut off before they were strangled to death. Their bodies were then hung up and used for target practice."[12]

---

[12] Name withheld for security reasons.

Both Jay and I were stunned and shocked by this account, and I was immediately reminded of the vision I had had the night before. The scriptures gives us some answers for the same hatreds and cruelties in evidence today that existed at the time of King David. Evil spirits don't die, they simply seek out new bodies to inhabit generation after generation. This explains the similarities of the deeds done today in comparison to those 3,000 years ago. This verse in the Book of Psalms,

> If I forget thee, O Jerusalem,
> let my right hand forget her cunning[13]

is rehearsed at every Jewish wedding. Could the cutting off of their right hands have any connection with Jerusalem being in the hands of the Jewish people today?

SABRA AND SHATILLA MASSACRE

An atmosphere of near despair enveloped Israel as a result of the tragic massacres at Sabra and Shatilla refugee camps near Beirut. For Christians living in Israel it was a revelation to see how much anger, frustration and self-incrimination engulfed this little nation. Yom Kippur, the Day of Atonement, when Jews repent and ask forgiveness, came only a few days after the massacre. The fresh shock of this tragedy and unrestrained vilification from the world made the Jewish Day of Atonement a time of anguished soul-searching for the entire nation. The 'Kahan Commission of Inquiry' was established in Israel and the results of their findings incriminated not only Israel for negligence, but the U.S.A. for pulling their troops out of the region two full weeks before the date previously agreed upon. The Christian Phalangist forces who had perpetrated the actual massacre in revenge for the assassination of their president-elect Bashir Gemayel, were found culpable. Finally, blame had to rest to some degree on the entire world community of nations that had turned a blind eye to the events occurring in Lebanon over the last eight years.

---

[13] Psalm 137:5

THE CHRISTIAN ENCLAVE

Major Saad Haddad administers an area called 'Free Lebanon'. Just south of Nabatiya this 20 kilometre wide strip of land is located between the Mediterranean coast on the west and Mt. Hermon on the east.

On Monday June 7, 1982, with an entourage of international press, local villagers, and Lebanese and Israeli soldiers looking on, Major Saad Haddad triumphantly planted the Free Lebanon flag at the peak of Beaufort Castle. It was an emotional moment for the 44 year old commander of the Christian enclave bordering Israel. Israeli troops had, after trying for years to eliminate the PLO stronghold in this ancient Crusader castle, seized Beaufort after a bitter hand to hand combat lasting nearly 12 hours. Major Haddad and his entire population in Free Lebanon were very grateful for the 'Operation Peace for Galilee' and the removal of the PLO threat in that area.

The Bible speaks in loving, poetic language concerning Lebanon. The fragrance that is Lebanon's or the nobility of its people, its waters, its streams and of course, its cedars. Peace flourished between Lebanon and Israel in the days of King David, Solomon and King Hiram. Cedars from Lebanon were used to build the temple in Jerusalem. Prophets Obadiah, Ezekiel and Amos lived and died in Lebanon. Jesus ministered in Zaraphat and Sidon. Unfortunately, the past is not present with us today. Lebanon sits in a ruin. But Major Haddad, this modern day man of God, is not discouraged. His words thrilled and encouraged the cosmopolitan audience of 3,500 Christians assembled at the 1982 Feast of Tabernacles in Jerusalem's Binyanei Ha'uma auditorium. He spoke the following words:

"Dear brothers and sisters in Jesus, I am coming from an isolated part of the world where we have all suffered greatly these past eight years. Without God's help it would have been impossible to hold on and survive. We were attacked day and night by terrorists. The terrorists didn't face any problems getting any weapons and ammunition from all over the fanatic Muslim world to make holy war against us 'infidels', as they call us, because we are Christians. The Communists did their best in sending all kinds of weapons, equipment and men. We were a very poor people fighting for our survival, land, dignity, creed and faith.

"Our children didn't enjoy their childhood as they spent most of their days in the shelters. Terrorists shelled them at school. We felt neglected and isolated, left alone by our Christian brothers all over the world. We had bitterness in our hearts knowing that the major powers of the world are in the hands of Christians . . . how could they just sit back and allow such a tragedy to go on for seven years against Christians. Even the Pope himself did nothing and said not a word in our favor. NO ONE intervened for Lebanon. Since 1860 many massacres have occurred in the Middle East against Christians, many churches were changed into mosques. St. John's Church in Damascus, where the grave of St. John is, remains a mosque to this day. During the last seven years in Lebanon many churches were used by the PLO as toilets.

"In all our history, we have never heard of the Jews working against the Christians. Unfortunately, that is not the history of Christianity, and God will show us how to wipe it away. We don't want history to describe the Lebanese as an ungrateful people. We are looking for a peace agreement not only because we love Israel, but as Christians we believe that our roots are in Judaism and most of our ancestors were Jews, therefore we all come from a common origin and we don't want to lose it. Our future as Christians is in danger. Arabic nations didn't want Lebanon ruled by a Christian president. Whatever the price they will renew their purposes to exterminate us.

"In all of these dark days we asked that God's word be spread not only in our area but in all of the Arabic countries. My hope was that maybe these people, on hearing the word of God, would stop destroying us. We prayed to have a radio station and again God intervened and sent us a good man named George Otis, founder of High Adventure Ministries. When he listened to me and my story, he said, 'You will get your radio station.' It's nice to be believed, but I said, 'It's impossible.'

"In a few weeks the radio station was established in the Valley of the Springs in Lebanon. It is the only radio station in the Middle East where the Bible is completely read four times a year. I want my people to hear the words of the Book, so that God can bring peace to their hearts and to the whole region. We know also that with the help of Mr. Pat Robertson the new CBN television station called Middle East Television will be working for the same purpose.

"We are a poor country with no oil, and anyone helping us would have had the oil embargo placed on them. When most Lebanese lost hope, God moved and made a miracle by asking Israel to intervene, and at that moment salvation came. The world described it as an invasion, we call it liberation. Where were all the other nations for seven years? Instead of thanking Israel for helping us and Lebanon and God, they accuse and blame her. Israel came to put the devil outside of Lebanon and not to harm any Lebanese citizens, or to claim any Lebanese territory. Go to Lebanon and ask her people, even Muslims, and they will tell you it was impossible to get rid of the terrorists without the intervention of Israel.

"You must be messengers to your countries. Ask your governments to work for peace between Lebanon and Israel. Thank you very much. I love you."[14]

> Is it not yet a very little while, and Lebanon shall be turned into a fruitful field, and the fruitful field shall be esteemed as a forest?
>
> And in that day shall the deaf hear the words of

[14] International Christian Celebration during the Feast of Tabernacles, tape recording, c/o I.C.E.J., Box 1192, Jerusalem, October 1982.

the book, and the eyes of the blind shall see out of obscurity, and out of darkness.

The meek also shall increase their joy in the Lord, and the poor among men shall rejoice in the Holy One of Israel.

For the terrible one is brought to nought, and the scorner is consumed, and all that watch for iniquity are cut off.[15]

---

[15] Isaiah 29:17–20

23

Within your Walls... Jerusalem

Fishers and Hunters would be incomplete without a place being made for the city of Jerusalem.

The fishers in this book have been involved in prophetic acts and have acted prophetically. Jerusalem is significant to millions of people as a prophetic city; a city waiting to be "visited from on high." Because of her spiritual importance Jerusalem is also called "the Time Clock of the World." Events taking place in this city set off chain reactions both spiritual and natural around the world.

We had lived four very happy and eventful years in Haifa but as we became more involved in making short television reports for Crossroads Christian Communications in Toronto, it became apparent that we needed to move to Jerusalem.

While contemplating where to begin searching for a place to live, Jay and I prayed and were given two very distinct impressions. The first was to surround ourselves with Jews and the second was to live within sight of the Temple Mount. We didn't understand the significance of this until after Jay answered an ad for an apartment in *The Jerusalem Post.* We drove up to Jerusalem for an interview with the landlord. We had not anticipated the surprise that awaited us. Much to our amazement he turned out to be a Rabbi living in the Jewish Quarter of the Old City.

The tassels of the Rabbi's prayer shawl hung over his blue jeans in a most contradictory manner. "Come, I want to show you something before we see the apartment," he said, leading us out of the door and into the narrow streets of the Jewish Quarter. We entered an ancient building that was in the process of being renovated into a Yeshiva. The Rabbi was responsible for the restoration project. "Elijah has been seen here," he announced with triumph in his voice. His hands lovingly touched the rough interior stone walls. Instead of being delighted with his news of Elijah, I felt edgy and frightened. "He thinks that we are Jews," I thought to myself. Turning to the Rabbi, I said, "You must know that we are Christians...."

His fiery eyes searched my face, and he broke into a broad grin. "I can see that you are a blessed people, so why do you make so much of it?" he asked, and dropped the subject. He led us to the new apartment, artistically designed to give optimal space and also commanding a sweeping view of the Temple Mount and the Mount of Olives. Jay and I knew that this was the place that we would call home.

A very special time in our lives began that day. It was the culmination of many years spent travelling to the Jewish communities in numerous countries around the world. Never, in our wildest imaginations, would we have considered such a beautiful and unique home in Jerusalem's heart. Joy and an overwhelming sense of homecoming filled us all. Armenians, Orthodox Christians, Muslims and Jews became our neighbors. The apartment was built over the top of an archeological site. Downstairs the walls dated back to the days of Hezekiah. Next door, "House of John Mark" was chisseled in aramaic on the corner stone dating back to the time of Christ. Upstairs the rooftop afforded us a 360-degree view of Jerusalem. The backdrop of the Temple Mount and the Mount of Olives provided a magnificent setting for TV interviews.

Using their Hebrew, the boys adjusted quickly and made new friends. After school they put on kippot and grabbed hammers and screwdrivers and went to help renovate the Yeshiva, only to return covered in dust and enthusiasm. Although children, they were having a tiny part in the building up of Zion. Today this Scripture is a reality for us: "For Thy servants take pleasure in her stones, and favour the dust thereof."[1]

In our spare time, we toured the newly excavated areas or walked the walls. On clear days we saw Herodion, a silent reminder of Herod's passion for privacy and splendor; off in the east, the mountains of Moab glimmered like a mirage in the heat. We talked about the hundreds of bullet holes which scar the face of Zion Gate, and were reminded that small boys fled through this gate in 1948 hugging ancient Torah scrolls. Four hundred years of Turkish rule ended when General Allenby walked through the Jaffa Gate in 1917. We stood on the Damascus Gate on a Friday morning to see the Muslim people stream through, dressed in their finest, on their way to worship. Next we visited the weekly sheep market on Friday mornings, where sheiks in flowing robes and turbans bartered over the price of sheep, goats and horses. St. Stephen's Gate was the key to Israel recovering the much-loved Western Wall during the Six-Day War in 1967.

The Golden Gate, otherwise known as the Gate of Mercy, remains unused, closed and silent, waiting.... As a family we rejoiced in our discoveries in Jerusalem. The biblical promise, "All your children shall be taught of the Lord," seemed a reality. Everywhere one's eyes rest in the Old City, they gaze upon some historical and biblical fact.

Jerusalem as seen with the natural eye is a hot dusty place. Summer sunshine reflects intense white light from hand-hewed stones. One longs for a cool shady tree to rest from the brilliance. Young Arab children sit in the dust, content to play

[1] Psalm 102:14.

with tiny stones or tin cans.... Jerusalem still has need of more playgrounds, parking lots and quietness. Her religious sons stride purposefully in the streets, a deep desire for God propelling them forward. Down in the markets, "Allo, allo" is the passing call to tourists. Lustful men stare at the continual stream of shapely young visitors. Stalls are piled high with produce from all over the land: grapes from Samaria, oranges and bananas from Jericho and vegetables from the Jezreel Valley. Almonds, cashews and pinenuts sit piled high in boxes alongside of chief spices too numerous to name. Fresh orange and carrot juice is sold from shops also offering colas or beer. Lamb meat roasting on the spit sends forth its succulent aroma, inviting one to "have a shuwarmah."

Shoemakers, tailors, basket weavers, butchers and bakers, metal workers, artists, rabbis, scribes, soldiers, stone workers, street sweepers and university professors are among our friends. My dressmaker is a devout Muslim, and during a fitting, it was not uncommon to see her stop work, put on a white Muslim covering and pray. Barefooted she knelt on a thin mat touching her forehead reverently to the floor.

Sunday evenings were special! One of our neighbors invited us to attend a Bible study class given by the oldest Rabbi in the Quarter. The Rabbi insisted on speaking Hebrew, and although he was frail of frame, his delightful sense of humor and insight into the Scriptures were a source of joy to us. He was the first Rabbi that we had met who cared very deeply about the Gentile peoples of the world. One evening as he was serving us tea and lemon cakes in his home, he paused, looked around the room, and in an apologetic manner said, "Please excuse my house, you see the light has gone out of it, for my dear wife of 50 years died just recently." What could one say to help ease his loss?

He readily accepted our invitation, and every other Sunday, came to our home. His long white beard gave him the appearance of an ancient patriarch. Ceremoniously he opened his Tanach, holding it in a respectful and careful manner. A deep longing welled up within me to communicate. In spite of our diverse backgrounds, we enjoyed a depth and flow of fellowship with him, that is not easily found. Later, as he stood in the doorway, about to leave, he smiled sweetly and then quoted Proverbs 27:19, "As in water face answereth to face, so the heart of man to man."

Other very special creatures existing under adverse circumstances inside of the Old City are cats. On the lookout for scraps they rear their young at the crossroads of the world.

We learned to discern a multitude of sounds. The stone walls of our building magnified the clanging of church bells ringing, muezzins calling from mosques to the faithful to pray five times a day, impatient car horns, jets breaking the sound barrier overhead, women arguing in Arabic, Aramaic or Hebrew, babies crying, the crisp clip-clop of donkeys loaded with cut stone, and the noise of energetic children who have come from around the world as promised by the prophets, to play in the streets of Jerusalem.

Just once we heard the blast of a bomb and felt tension and hostility rise. Shops were boarded up. The streets were emptied and people spoke in whispers, as soldiers patrolled. Terror has many faces.

Feet from all over the world have walked these narrow stone streets. Babylonians, Persians, Assyrians, Greeks, Romans, Byzantines, Muslims, Crusaders, Turks and British came to conquer and rule in the past. Delegates from the United Nations Peace-Keeping Forces are here today. Death has visited time after time, yet it cannot keep life from continuing to spring forth within Jerusalem.

In preparation for the Sabbath, Ephraim, our neighbor, washes down the narrow street that runs past our door. As shadows lengthen and the Shabbat approaches, expectation rises. Perhaps the Messiah's footsteps will be heard this holy night. Peace descends as the Sabbath rest begins. We walked together as a family down to the Western Wall, with our observant neighbors. One senses that God's Presence hovers over this sacred place, setting it and the people who pray there apart for Himself.

Bathed in golden light at sunset, the stones become warm, alive and responsive. Prayer is a most natural and spontaneous response, taking us back to the days of David's Tabernacle. Scribes recorded the anointed prayers sung to sweet music that were dedicated to The Holy One of Israel on this mountain.

Quietness enters one's soul in remembering that most of God's great men found in the Bible lived here, their futures intrinsically bound up with your own Jerusalem... Melchizedek, Abraham, David, Isaiah, Jeremiah, Ezekiel, Daniel, Nehemiah, Jesus ... to this day your noble line continues throughout the earth.

Prayer has become a way of life, flowing from our minds and hearts effortlessly, the result of living within your walls! We will "...give Him no rest, till He establish, and till He make Jerusalem a praise in the earth."[2]

"Pray for the peace of Jerusalem, they shall prosper that love thee. Peace be within thy walls, and prosperity within thy palaces."[3]

Bowing in prayer, the heart's cries of the centuries fill our ears, our souls... the cry is exactly the same today, reaching up to You O Holy One from this place.

Jerusalem has a mother's heart, and loves all of her children. She has room for everyone.

Earthly cares fade away even now as we think about the days awaiting us... days of peace.

We have touched your heart, Jerusalem, and by praying for your peace and your peoples we have come close to the Almighty.

---

[2] Isaiah 62:7.

[3] Psalm 122:6, 7.

Jerusalem,
how many years you have waited
to be... visited from on high,
dressed in Royal Apparel,
to rejoice in the dance.
Your Peace; crown of all the earth.

Messiah,
only You will make war cease,
oh . . . Righteous Prince of Peace,
come, wipe away all tears
superstition, pain and fear.
Your crown; Shalom for all the earth.

JERUSALEM

24
Ethiopian Outcasts

"For our soul is bowed down to the dust: our belly cleaveth unto the earth. Arise for our help, and redeem us for thy mercies' sake."
Psalm 44:25

"Ethiopia is God's way of putting an end to things."
This tragic yet prophetic line was written by an Ethiopian novelist some years before the drought and famine began its devastation of north-east Africa. According to the U.N. over 150 million Africans are being affected by the longest drought and famine in recent history. The Nile River, the lifeline for a great part of the continent, is at its lowest level in living memory. And for great masses of people disaster is not imminent, but present. Sudan, Africa's largest country geographically, is buckling under the strain of the hundreds of thousands of refugees pouring in from Ethiopia, Chad and Uganda. Some of these refugees are Falashas, or Ethiopian Jews.

The heat is unbearable. In summer the temperature rises to 130 degrees. Horrific refugee camps exist on the Sudan — Ethiopia border where 85,000 people in one camp alone are crowded together in make-shift shelters. Smoke from cooking fires mingles with a permanent cloud of powdery dust that hangs in the air between the straw huts. In every direction one hears the sound of crying, wailing and coughing. Pneumonia and endemic dysentry are two of the big killers of multitudes weakened by years of starvation. Everywhere is wretchedness and dirt. People die like flies. One body after another is carried through the camps on stretchers. Make-shift graves of rock-piles and sand pepper the ground surrounding each camp, a grim illustration of death's toll.

Sudan and Ethiopia, countries struggling out of the Middle Ages, are incapable of withstanding the earth-shaking tragedies that have befallen them. Billions of dollars and 10,000 Western volunteers are the only hope for these millions who are facing death, according to relief officials, field workers and diplomats.

James Grant, the international director of UNICEF said, "Even if there had been no major drought, four and a half million African kids under the age of four would have died this year." . . . "The drought may kill another million people."

February 1st, 1985 Jerusalem Post

In its first thirty years the Jewish national home, Israel, absorbed hundreds of thousands of Jewish refugees. Most had fled from Arab countries. More than 100,000 were survivors of the Nazi concentration camps and tens of thousands of others managed to flee from repressive post-war regimes of the left and right. Israel also attracted a small number of Western Jews who might have suffered social anti-semitism, but who couldn't be considered as refugees, or victims of authoritarian rule. In all Israel absorbed 1,700,000 Jews from more than seventy counries, Moroccans, Russians, Kurds, Indians, Bulgarians, Iraquis, Swedes, Peruvians, Iranians, Georgians, Rhodesians, Germans, Americans and Yemenites, to name a few. No major effort was ever made to bring Ethiopian Jews to Israel, although over the years about 300 had made their own way there.

When Menachem Begin became Prime Minister in 1977 he resolved to bring the Ethiopian Jews to Israel. But after two plane loads arrived the operation was aborted following a 'slip of the tongue' by the then foreign minister Moshe Dayan. The immigration effort was renewed three years ago and in recent months it was speeded up by Prime Minister Shimon Peres and his predecessor, Yizhak Shamir. In 1984 Israel absorbed 20,000 new immigrants, many of them Ethiopian Jews. In the last two months of 1984 and January 1985 many more were airlifted to Israel, until Prime Minister Shimon Perez made an official statement to the press concerning this latest aliyah. Two days later the air lifts stopped and as far as we know have not continued. It is believed that the current total population of Ethiopian Jews worldwide is between 26,000 and 28,000. Today there are 10,000 to 11,000 in Israel, 1,500 to 3,000 in refugee camps in the Sudan, and the rest are locked inside Ethiopia. As mentioned the conditions are appalling and thousands have died of starvation and disease.

The Ethiopian Jews call themselves 'Beta Israel' or the 'House of Israel'. They regard the term 'Falasha' as a derogatory word, or an Ethiopian slave name meaning 'stranger' or 'exile' which is how the tribe has been perceived since ancient times. The tribe's origin is shrouded in mystery, and there are at least a dozen theories about where it came from and how and when it acquired its Judaic beliefs.

Jerusalem Post January 6th 1985

Leading rabbis over the last five centuries have identified the Ethiopian Jews as the Lost Tribe of Dan, one of the Ten Tribes carried away when the Assyrians destroyed the northern kingdom of Israel in 772 B.C. Secular scholars say the Beta Israel are probably descendants of converts and that they learned their Judaism from merchants travelling from nearby Yemen to the tribe's home in the mountainous region north of Lake Tana, source of the Blue Nile. Scholars believe they are related to the Agau tribes, Ethiopia's indigenous people. According to one Jewish tradition, they are the progeny of King Solomon and an Ethiopian queen. Some scholars say that the Beta Israel were converted 2,500 years ago by the Jewish soldiers garrisoned on the island of Elephantine on the Nubian-Egyptian border, some 800 kilometers from present Beta Israel country.

These black Jews have no rabbinic tradition. They study the

Torah in 'Ge'ez' an ancient holy language that only the priests learn. It is thought to be a semitic language as is Amharic, the national language of Ethiopia. They have a priesthood or 'cohanim' who claim descent from Aaron, brother of Moses. Until recently they practised pre-Talmudic Judaism indicating that they acquired their Jewish beliefs at least 2,000 years ago, before the Roman destruction of the Second Temple.

After a 400 year war the Beta Israel, who once numbered in the hundreds of thousands were defeated and reduced to slavery. They were forbidden to own land and this edict was in force, with a handful of exceptions, until the overthrow of Emperor Haile Selassie in 1974. Throughout the last five centuries they have been despised objects of superstition and suffered intense persecution at the hands of their Christian and Muslim neighbours. Their numbers dwindled to about 30,000. Recently, according to a group of American and Canadian Jews who visited the Jewish area of Gondar in Ethiopia, a brutal provincial governor, a Major Malaku, closed off Falasha villages to all outsiders and intensified the persecution of these despised peoples. Children have been murdered in front of their parents, and old people have been thrown on cruel thorn bushes and left to die. As a result Falashas are still begging for salvation. The words of the prophet Zephaniah carry an eternal ring of reality.

"From beyond the rivers of Ethiopia my suppliants, even the daughter of my dispersed, shall bring mine offering."

Zephaniah 3:10

In 1975, two years after Sephardi Chief Rabbi Ovadia Yosef ruled that the Beta Israel were members of the Lost Tribe of Dan and were entitled to be redeemed, the Israel government officially recognized the tribe as Jewish, and thereby entitled them to Israeli citizenship under the Law of Return. This was the beginning of the modern miracle of their return.

The new arrivals came to Israel much like those from the Holocaust, naked and bare-foot. The government provided shoes and jackets immediately upon arrival, as the cool Israeli winter was a drastic change from the sweltering heat of Sudan's refugee camps. Local Israeli citizens responded wonderfully to pleas made in the newspapers and on television and radio by overloading the dozens of absorption centers in Israel with such an abundance of clothing that the officials had to cry, "Enough, bring no more."

Before being sent to the various centres, from the Galilee in the north to Eilat in the south, each Ethiopian underwent extensive medical examinations and treatment. They received relief from malaria, intestinal worms and parasites. Most are deficient nutritionally and carry many related diseases. Some of the diseases they sustain have been seen by Israeli doctors only in their medical text books. The widespread eye diseases of Ethiopia present a major concern, while mobile dental clinics, on loan from the Israel Defence Forces, visit the absorption centres throughout the country.

Repeatedly we had heard how religious these black Jews were and a good illustration of their devotion to the Mosaic law took place at Jerusalem's Share Zedek hospital on a Sabbath. As usual, at meal time, trays of warm nutritious food were brought to the patients, which included many Ethiopians. Not one of the Africans touched the food, but instead sat in a horrified silence until Rabbis were summoned. The conflict was over warm food! How could you warm food on the Sabbath and not have broken the law by kindling a fire? The Rabbis patiently explained that they have new devices for the express purpose of keeping the food warm over the Sabbath. The Ethiopians were encouraged to eat and assured that they would not be sinning. Silently they continued to sit . . . until the food grew cold and then they ate it with relish. I have heard Israelis say "They are more religious than we are."

High priest of the Beta Israel tribe, seventy-seven year old Arye Ben David, cited a prophecy from Isaiah to explain the events that were happening to his tribe, the Jews of Ethiopia. After the exodus from Egypt the Lord would "set his hand a second time" and this second exodus would "recover the remnant of His people that shall remain from Assyria (Syria), and from Egypt, Pathos (Upper Egypt) and from Cush (Ethiopia), . . . and He will assemble the dispersed of Israel (the ten lost tribes) and gather together the scattered of Judah from the four corners of the earth."

(Page 230, The Lost Jews, Louis Rapoport.)

To most of the new arrivals in Israel their culture shock is intense. Many had never been outside of their remote villages in the Ethiopian highlands and couldn't imagine what magic would confront them in Israel. They are taught from scratch about the exotic implements for cooking that use mysterious 'gas' which is especially hard to explain. They don't know how dangerous it is and may leave it on all night. A constant check has to be kept. The food is also a very big problem. No 'teff' — their staple grain — grows in Israel so they are taught to make a local version of 'injerra', Ethiopian bread, out of wheat flour. They are fed potatoes and rice at every meal until they are able to tolerate the new tastes of Israeli food.

Water, hot and cold, at one's fingertips is a marvellous invention to women and girls who as beasts of burden for centuries lugged huge clay pots of water from far springs or wells to their huts. Some have deformed spines from this very hard labour. To an Ethiopian peasant whose mud dwelling has no opening other than a single door the glassy tile floors, windows in walls and toilets are as foreign to their feudal society as their mud huts would be to us.

Situations have arisen that require patience and understanding. According to Jewish law, when a woman menstruates she is considered unclean. In Ethiopia she would take up residence in a small hut away from the main dwelling during the days of her uncleanness. What is a woman to do, living in the confines of a small Israeli apartment? Older Ethiopian women have been found sitting for days under the central stairwell of the apartment building waiting out the duration of their period of uncleaness separated from their households, not wanting to break the law.

Recently we were sent two large boxes of soap, shampoo, hand cream, cologne, combs and baby clothes from America. Everyone in Israel was following the daily news with great interest to learn about our latest arrivals. In prayer I had seen these Ethiopians represented as a small helpless child, being lovingly held in the arms of Israel. I saw Israel as a mother, and was impressed that as a nation she was exhibiting tenderness and kindness to her returned kinsmen, something so close and touching to the very heart of God. With these boxes of goodies I now had a perfect opportunity to visit the absorption center for new immigrants just around the block from our home. When speaking with the social worker in charge and upon hearing that I had boxes of goods, her response was immediate "Oh thank you, but we don't need any more clothes. In fact we have to have trucks come and take away so much of it."

"No," I explained, "we have cosmetic items!" Her countenance brightened as I showed her the beautifully wrapped gifts. There was more than enough for the 28 families there. We carried the boxes inside the community centre, whose walls were lined with tables, piled high with clothing. She shared that just recently Ethiopian children received gifts of black dolls from American Jews, after a New Yorker read in the Jerusalem Post that the youngsters were frightened of white dolls, never having seen them before. A group of tourists brought the 400 black dolls in their suitcases.

"This has been a project of love", one lady explained. "Each new immigrant family here from America or Europe has adopted an Ethiopian family and is helping them to adjust."

Gleaning any current information on the situation of the Ethiopian Jews still in Ethiopia or the Sudan is almost impossible. Officials are tight lipped as the lives of thousands hang in the balance. I was further delighted to have a second peek into the lives of our new Israelis and joined a group of interested American Jews on a trip to a co-operative moshav six miles east of Natanya on the coast. This centre has just been opened to house 88 Ethiopian youths from separated families, who had arrived on the latest airlift. The wide-eyed young people were 18 to 26 years of age and were devoting their time entirely to study. Fifty percent were literate and some had completed grades eleven and twelve. They are now in full-time Hebrew classes, six days a week and learn the geography of Israel and Judaism in the afternoons. Evenings are spent learning folk dances, playing sports, or watching movies, and taking trips throughout their new home land. Everything is interpreted from Hebrew into Amharic, their native tongue. All had chosen Hebrew names when they arrived, while a few were given Bible names from birth.

At home in the hills of Ethiopia almost everyone works all of their lives in agriculture, but our guide said, "Their thirst for knowledge and their intelligence is amazing. They are very highly motivated and desire above all else to learn. They don't want to have anything to do with farming or agriculture."

On this moshav these quiet but determined Zionists will spend ten months in prevocational programs, followed by two months of intensified training which will enable them to work in factories or laboratories where they will receive on-the-job training. A few want to go on to university. There are nine or ten similar centres throughout Israel especially for the Ethiopian youth who arrive without families.

Eighteen young people sat with their desks in a semi-circle. The Hebrew class was in session around the blackboard covered with Hebrew lettering and their teacher was a young vivacious Israeli, dressed unceremoniously in tight jeans. By way of contrast the Ethiopian girls were modestly outfitted in dresses and skirts. I had to smile at the high heels worn by some who just a few weeks before had arrived barefoot. Proudly yet shyly they lifted their notebooks up for our inspection. Their written work was meticulous. We were sensitive not to take any pictures which would in any way make them feel like oddities.

Israel and her citizens are to be commended for the care and nurture they are lavishing upon one of her lost tribes. I was seeing history and prophecy entwined before my eyes, for as boldly commanded by Isaiah the prophet so many thousands of years ago, the 'South' was not able to keep them back. One visitor in our group, a well-to-do Jewess from Florida, fashionably dressed with expensive jewellery, covered her tears by putting on dark glasses. She concluded our visit by whispering, "I'm very touched when I think about this miracle."

The Ethiopian Jews believe that they have been delivered from a land of famine and pestilence and returned to their ancestral homeland. They see it in terms of a miracle on the road to redemption and an answer to prayers which they have recited every day for thousands of years in exile. But there is also great sorrow for the thousands who have died of disease and starvation, and consternation over the fact that the story of the operation of their deliverance has been revealed before all of the Ethiopian Jews are safely in Israel.

Both the Fishers and the Hunters are clearly exemplified in this unfolding saga of Ethiopian Jewry.

Glossary

Achshav: now

Aliyah: immigration of Jews to Israel

Ani Ma'amin: I believe

Baruch Ha-Shem: 'Blessed is the Name'

Boker Tov: good morning

Brit Hadashah: New Testament

Chutzpah: nerve, cheek, impudent behavior

Korban: 'that which is brought near,' sacrifice

Dati: religious

Diaspora: dispersion of Jews throughout the world

Dovening: Jewish custom of bowing from waist during prayer

El Shaddai: Name meaning Almighty God or double-breasted one

Goyim: Gentiles

Gush Emunim: Group of the faithful—those who believe in settling biblical Israel

Hassidic: Orthodox, pious or righteous Jew

Haver, Haverim: friend, friends

Kaporeh: atonement

Kiddush: prayer of sanctification recited over wine on Sabbaths and festivals

Kipah: skull cap

Kibbutzim: collective farms in Israel

Kosher: ritually clean or pure

Kotel: retaining Western Wall of The Second Temple

Jeshua Ha-Mashiah: Jesus the Messiah

Macumba: Brazil's religious practice of black magic

Magen David: the Star of David

Mashiah: Messiah

Minyan: the minimum number of Jewish men required for prayer, ten

Mishpahah: family

Mitzvah: commandment which has evolved to mean a good deed

Moreh: teacher

Moshav: communal agricultural settlement with varying degrees of free enterprise and private ownership

Muharabeen: an Arabic word for Destroyers or Destructors

Ruach Ha-Kodesh: Holy Spirit

Seder: Passover meal

Shul: Yiddish for synagogue

Sabra: a Jew born in Israel

Shabbat: Sabbath or seventh day of the week

Shaliah: one who is sent to encourage aliyah

Tefillin: phylacteries

Ulpan: Hebrew-language school

Yom Kippur: Day of Atonement

INTERNATIONAL VISTAS

Headquarters – Israel
Box 8232, Jerusalem 91081
Tel. (02) 246027
Telex 26144 BXJMIL ext. 7276

Great Britain
c/o New Wine Press
PO Box 17
Chichester, W Sussex

European Donations
Account No. 162008
Stadtsparkasse Frankfurt/Main, Germany
BLZ 50050102

USA
Box 24630
Dallas, Texas 75224
Tel. (214) 9483411

Canada
243 Broadway
Orangeville, Ontario L9W 1K6
Tel. (519) 9414310

South Africa
PO Box 2212
Honeydew
2040 Johannesburg,
Rep. of S. Africa

Please find enclosed my prepaid order.

BOOKS (postage & handling add $1.00 per book)

☐ "FISHERS AND HUNTERS". Visits to Jewish communities around the world encouraging them to return to Zion.
Large format edition US$6.95 Abridged edition US$3.95

☐ "GATES OF BRASS". On the plight of Soviet Jews including secret material smuggled out of Russia. The 'behind the scenes' story to the film production by the same title.
US$5.95

CASSETTE MESSAGES

☐ "WE WILL NOT BE SILENT" *US$3.00*

☐ "REPORT ON TRIP INTO USSR" *US$3.00*

FILMS & VIDEOS (postage & handling add $2.00)

☐ "APPLES OF GOLD" Modern History of Israel (78 min.)

Film		US$995
½" Video	☐ VHS	US$85
	☐ BETA	US$85

☐ "GATES OF BRASS" Plight of Soviet Jews, "Let My People Go"
Film Project. (54 min.)

½" Video	☐ VHS	US$75
	☐ BETA	US$75

☐ "LEBANON AND THE MIDDLE EAST – THE UNTOLD STORY (28 min.)

½" Video	☐ VHS	US$55
	☐ BETA	US$55

☐ Message on Plight of Soviet Jews – "Refuseniks" with exclusive film interviews from the USSR. 45 min.

½" Video	☐ VHS	US$35
	☐ BETA	US$35

Amount enclosed:

Name

Address